PRAISE FOR *THE MANNA PARADIGM SHIFT:*

"This book is a game changer. It contains a powerful interpretation of an ancient mystical teaching that will support you in creating a new consciousness of abundance and freedom."

—**Dr. Shefali Tsabary,** psychologist, spiritual teacher, and author of The Conscious Parent

"As a Toltec wisdom teacher, I understand the power of applying ancient knowledge to our lives. Psychologist Davina Kotulski has recovered a sacred teaching from the Near East and developed an inspired approach to apply it to the rhythms and realities of the modern lifestyle. This book is a must-read for anyone interested in personal transformation."

—**HeatherAsh Amara,** author of Warrior Goddess Training and The Warrior Heart Practice

"In a time of loss, fear, and lack, The Manna Paradigm Shift will help you ascend all obstacles and take your power back. Dr. Davina is the real deal! This book will open you to a world of possibility."

—**Sky Cowans,** video creator, social media influencer, and founder of Sky Life

"In times of great uncertainty, it is important to connect with the wisdom of the ages. That's why I teach about the elements and am drawn to shamanic wisdom. It's also why I feel aligned to Dr. Davina Kotulski's new book. Dr. Kotulski, a psychologist and spiritual practitioner, applies the ancient Judaic teaching of manna from heaven to create an inspired mindset that will help you navigate these turbulent times and keep moving forward."

—**Renee Baribeau,** Hay House author of Winds of Spirit

"In The Manna Paradigm Shift, Davina Kotulski has given a simple and empowering way to go from limited scarcity thinking to a consciousness of abundance and limitless possibilities. She knows how to take you from the wilderness desert mentality into the land of plenty if you are willing to make the gentle mental changes that lead to a new attitude. If you can change your thinking, you can change your life. This book will show you how. Now, get started and see for yourself what miracles happen when you step out of worn-out, limiting beliefs and into a new paradigm of possibilities!"

—**Jacob Glass,** spiritual teacher and author of
The Miracle Worker's Handbook

"I wholeheartedly recommend The Manna Paradigm Shift. Through these unprecedented times of challenges, new directions and visions for our lives present themselves to us, and more often than not, with questions. How do we balance security with our hearts' desires? How do we move forward toward a horizon that seems to be slipping away? From the first page, this book describes the path forward and sets forth the steps to fulfill the soul's purpose in a clear and understandable way. I felt supported and understood by Dr. Kotulski as I flowed through the pages. It was if I was with her at the kitchen table as she was talked to me as a treasured friend. I loved the book!"

—**Flicka Rahn**, associate professor of music (retired), Texas A&M University, sound therapist, composer, and author of The Transformational Power of Sound and Music

"At the heart of The Manna Paradigm Shift is the message that we can trust our needs are being taken care of. The psychological processes in this book are remarkable. So clear and straightforward. They help create a sense of security that allows us to move forward in the face of adversity and uncertainty. I love it!"

—**Paul Bartholomew**, actor and announcer for The Ellen Show

"We all want to be awake in our lives and our work. We all want to feel whole. Dr. Davina Kotulski's beautiful new book The Manna Paradigm Shift teaches an ancient principle for accomplishing these goals. The combination of psychology and spirituality in the method she teaches is truly empowering. Daily practice of the manna mindset principles will build a strong foundation for your life."

—**Sam Liebowitz**, author of Everyday Awakening

"The Manna Paradigm Shift is the book to read right now if you're seeking inspired and practical ideas for manifesting greater peace and abundance. Dr. Davina Kotulski shares from her years of experience in counseling and praying with clients from all walks of life. The 30-Day Manna Challenge offers a practical plan for incorporating the manna paradigm shift into your own life."

—Cheryl Leutjen, author of Love Earth Now

"The Manna Paradigm Shift by Davina Kotulski is an incredibly powerful and well-written book that will encourage you to liberate yourself by overcoming limiting beliefs and shifting into an empowered mindset. It offers life-changing insights and practical tools that will assist you in connecting with your higher consciousness, elevating your frequency, and stepping into a life of greater freedom and abundance."

—TJ Woodward, bestselling author, inspirational speaker, and recovery specialist

THE MANNA PARADIGM SHIFT

CREATING THE CONSCIOUSNESS OF ABUNDANCE AND FREEDOM

DAVINA KOTULSKI, PH.D.

Red Ink
PRESS

LOS ANGELES, CALIFORNIA

Davina Kotulski / Red Ink Press
www.davinakotulski.com

Copy editing and production by Stephanie Gunning
Cover design by Gus Yoo
Book Layout © Book Design Templates

Special discounts are available on quantity purchases by corporations, associations, and others. For details, contact the publisher at the address or website above.

Library of Congress Control Number: 2020923152

The Manna Paradigm Shift/ Davina Kotulski. —1st ed.
ISBN 978-0-9978379-6-4 (paperback)

To Diana

THE MANNA MINDSET
MANIFESTO

"I choose freedom. I am a sovereign being, free from enslavement. I have a direct connection with the Source of all life. The Universe is my source and sufficiency in all things. All of my needs are met by the Universe in perfect timing. I receive manna from heaven daily, and I am grateful."

CONTENTS

FOREWORD

∾

DR. SHEFALI TSABARY

It is clear that we need a paradigm shift in our world. It is clear that we have stepped into a severe abyss of pain and fear. The only way out of this morass is a shift in consciousness. This is where this book you are holding in your hands is going to be of huge help.

This book by psychologist Davina Kotulski, Ph.D., is a game changer. In its pages lie lessons of tremendous value and healing. This book contains a powerful interpretation of an ancient mystical teaching that will support you in creating a new consciousness of abundance and freedom.

Everyone wants to know how to attract more abundance and freedom, but few know how to lay it out in a systematic manner. This is what this book offers: practical steps that each of us can follow that will lead us to greater alignment with our highest purpose and vision. You will learn specific actions to uplift your consciousness in these challenging times so that you can enter into a new, sovereign state of being. You will understand how common practices like competition, hoarding, and excessive doing diminish the soul's true path and how rest and present-moment living rejuvenate and inspire us into our highest calling.

The Manna Paradigm Shift will transform how you live your life. When you begin living by principles of manna, and not by greed for money, your life will truly shift. Dr. Davina's simple yet powerful way of teaching empowers us to take our power back from traditions, corporations, gurus, politicians, fads, and society. She teaches us not to fear change and, instead, how to flow with it. Through her words, you will learn to embrace your struggles and learn from them. She will gift you the power of insight and courage so that you no longer resist the teachings from your life, but instead transform them into wisdom and vision.

The system is broken. It's always been broken, but now, post-corona, we can see just how flawed the old ways were. Dr. Davina's book offers you a pathway through the rubble. It creates hope.

We need a book like this today as we deal with the heightened manipulations of the world. This book will help you set yourself free. After all, all we have power over is ourselves: our growth, our sanity, our evolution forward. This book will give you just the inspiration and empowerment you need to make those changes you have always yearned for. I hope you allow its teachings to shift and move you deeply.

INTRODUCTION

෨෧

*Learning the ancient truth of manna can qualitatively
change your life.*

I spotted my supervisor, David, walking briskly across
the parking lot. I was on my way to lunch and had asked
him several times for a private meeting.

It was apparent he was in a hurry. It didn't matter to
me. I knew that if I didn't say it now, it would only be
harder later. I chased after him and mustering all my
courage, I insisted, "David, I need to speak to you."

He probably imagined I was going to express my
frustration over the ground squirrels in the parking lot
that were constantly chewing on the wiring in my car
and had already cost me $1,500 —three separate $500
deductible payments on my auto insurance. Or maybe
he imagined I wanted to complain about the fact that one
of my psychology interns, a legal immigrant who had
possessed a valid green card for over a decade, still didn't
have computer access to the online psych files because
of a new restriction limiting computer access to U.S.
citizens only.

"I'm going to resign, and I'm giving three months' notice," I said. Whatever he imagined, I'm sure he never expected me to say that.

"You're stupid," he blurted out. Whatever I imagined, I never expected him to say that. I had figured he would try to talk me out of my decision for a whole host of reasons. My own inner voice was already filling me with doubt and yammering on about how crazy my decision was.

I had worked for the U.S. Department of Justice for thirteen years as a psychologist at the Federal Correctional Complex in Dublin, California. A year previously, I had been honored as the employee of the year for my commitment to providing excellent mental health services to female inmates. I made close to six figures, with more than four weeks of paid vacation, federal holidays off, and a requirement that I did not work more than forty hours a week

We stood between two parked SUVs. The noonday September sun beat down on us, adding to the heat of the scolding he gave me. "This is a great job, and in just over a dozen years, you can retire, which means you'll have benefits for the rest of your life," David said.

I knew all of this. These were the very thoughts I had put aside to take the leap of faith to give my notice.

I understood why he looked incredulous. David was a good man. He cared about me and was concerned that I was making a terrible decision. Yet, I was clear that staying would ultimately prove to be a more stupid thing to do with my one precious life.

Two years before, I had been filling an officer's post in the Special Housing Unit. The Special Housing Unit called the SHU, or more commonly "The Hole," is where inmates are locked down twenty-three hours a day. Inmates in the SHU get one hour of recreation time in an outdoor cage. Since we were short-staffed, I had to cancel my therapy groups and go help cuff the SHU inmates and take them from their cell to the recreation area. These were people I would be giving therapy to, and here I was expected to handcuff them. The lieutenant I was working with thought I was taking too long to get the cuffs on and off the inmates. He also didn't care much for psychologists, so he had me reassigned, and I was sent to work an armed patrol post.

Every year at the prison, staff had to requalify their weapons skills. I had several years of firearms training under my belt and was proficient with a shotgun, a 9mm handgun, and an M-16 assault rifle. Though all staff members, regardless of position, were considered correctional workers first, I was told when hired, that I would only have to work armed posts in emergencies. This was not an emergency. I did not want to be assigned to a post where, potentially, I would have to shoot or kill someone. I asked to be reassigned.

I was denied.

I went to my supervisor and then up the chain of the command to the captain, then the warden, all the way to the regional psychology administrator. I repeated the stipulation that psychologists were only required to work armed posts in emergencies. I was told, "Get your ass in the truck, or you're going to get beach time." *Beach time* is slang for unpaid administrative leave.

I felt helpless and defeated as I walked back toward the prison's exit. I passed the chaplain on my way. "I did not become a psychologist to shoot people," I told him. He sympathized. Chaplains were the only employees exempt from this kind of duty.

Just as I received the truck keys and was getting ready to holster my 9mm, I received a call on the radio. One of the correctional staff members at the minimum-security prison camp across the street had heard about my request and agreed to switch posts. I was extremely grateful.

And yet, my face burned with humiliation as I worked the officer's post at the prison camp. I sorted mail and did the other correctional tasks, while also trying to provide supervision to a psych intern on her clinical cases. I couldn't stop thinking about what had been demanded of me. It unnerved me that I had so little control over my own moral compass and freedom. To suddenly realize that I didn't have a choice over whether or not to work an armed post where I might have to shoot or kill someone cut me to the core. That wasn't the situation I had signed up for. But I felt like I couldn't just quit and walk away because I had a mortgage to pay. They owned me. I had to do what they said or else.

After that day, I tried to move forward. I buried my feelings. I continued to work hard and got recognition for my service. Yet I never felt settled. I kept getting repeated callings and intuitive nudges and taps that I needed to stop infusing the federal government with the ultimate power over my well-being. I began to feel that this great government job was actually keeping me stuck in ways that I couldn't articulate. My priorities and values had changed over the years. Trading days of my life for my government paycheck was proving more costly every day.

I felt I needed to put my faith in a greater power. Recognizing that I had to take off the golden handcuffs and set myself free, I decided I would start a private practice. I would see clients on my terms and in a way that was meaningful to me. No more compromises and endless workplace politics.

That conversation in the parking lot with David was my declaration of freedom. At that moment, I chose faith over finances.

I didn't know then that there would be many more moments like that to come.

I could have taken his words as an insult, but I didn't. I knew he was looking out for me based on his own fears, not mine.

David shrugged his shoulders and walked away in disbelief.

The very next day—and I do mean the *very* next day—the news announced that our nation was in a recession. It was September 13, 2008.

"You're not going to quit now that we're in a recession, right?" people reasoned with me. As the days passed, the flow of information concerning the seriousness of the recession increased. David and my coworkers became convinced I'd reverse my decision. After all, who in their right mind would leave a stable job with an excellent salary at the onset of an economic crash?

The *logical* thing would have been to stay.

I didn't have any clients yet. No job awaited me in the wings. In fact, this was the first time in my life I wasn't working multiple jobs and had no backup plan. What could possibly cause me to quit at a moment like this?

But recession or not, there was no way I was going to change my mind, and I told this to everyone who suggested it to me. I was choosing freedom.

Through the experience of making this leap and thriving, I learned that the Universe would meet my needs one day at a time as I shifted my consciousness. As I learned how to lean into the ancient truth of manna, it qualitatively changed my life. Since then, I've been passionate about helping others make this shift so they too could experience a deeper quality of freedom and abundance.

We Need a New Normal

The old way isn't working, and it hasn't for a long time. Too many people feel anxious about their financial situations, concerned about their healthcare and afraid for their future. Life feels too uncertain.

Most people who come to me for therapy, life coaching, or spiritual counseling are struggling with these things as well. They want more freedom and joy in their lives, but they feel weighed down by work obligations and financial fears. Perhaps you do, too.

You want the freedom to make choices for your life. You want to travel. You want to spend more time with your loved ones, your children, and your family. You want to enjoy creative pursuits. You want to just relax and reconnect with friends. You want to feel free to be yourself and live a life that reflects your values.

But you're not.

You don't have *enough*. Enough money. Enough time. You are tethered to your phone. Your laptop. The line between your work-life and home-life has vanished.

You don't have energy to keep up with life's demands. You may feel like your employer owns you. You may hate your job, but you can't imagine how things could get any better.

We have all felt held hostage by financial demands and work obligations, terrified to make changes.

The current model has us put our faith in something outside of ourselves: corporations, governments, financial markets, the almighty dollar. It takes away our power. We find ourselves caught up in a system that requires more and more effort to make a living, leaving us to lease our lives on weekends and vacations. It robs our children of our time and attention.

This is especially true for Americans. According to Samuel P. Harrington, author of *Who Are We? The Challenges to America's National Identity,* Americans "work longer hours, have shorter vacations, get less in unemployment, disability, and retirement benefits, and retire later than people in comparably rich societies."[1]

Our current economic paradigm, which puts *profit before people,* is terrible for our bodies and our health. Overwork and stress lead to health problems, including insomnia, depression, substance abuse, heart disease, and diabetes. Our materialism keeps us fixated on the accumulation of possessions over our quality of life. Ironically, our need to pay insurance premiums and maintain healthcare has us acting in ways that are detrimental to our well-being.

This isn't what we want, but it's what we're familiar with.

This system separates us from our real power. It's a system that runs and profits on fear. That fear is fueled by the widespread economic disparity growing every day in our country and worldwide. We are creating an ever-larger servant class.

We are in bondage unable to freely live our lives.

We need a new normal.

The Manna Paradigm Shift

I want to introduce you to a new way of living that will create something better for yourself and others. *The Manna Paradigm Shift* will help you follow the flow and create an abundant life one day at a time. This mindset is based on a concept I developed over many years of working with people who were feeling anxious and depressed, restless, burned out, or stuck. It helps you put the focus back on what you can control—your consciousness.

The Manna Paradigm Shift will help you create a manna mindset and stay in manna consciousness—a mindset of positive expectancy, focusing on personal agency, gratitude, and appreciation. Rather than being overcome by a mentality of scarcity and giving up personal power to corporations, politicians, and the economic system, the concepts and practices in *The Manna Paradigm Shift* will help you bring your power back to the Source within you.

Based on the ancient parable of manna from heaven, *The Manna Paradigm Shift* will teach you how to listen deeply to the guidance given to you by your higher consciousness moment by moment, day by day. As you learn how to tap into this ancient spiritual knowledge, you'll connect with a power greater than fear so that you can experience more freedom and fulfillment in your life. Making this shift in your mentality will help you stay present in the Presence, so you can make wise choices and stay focused on what is, not what was, or what will be. It will help you find ways to act from faith rather than fear.

The word *manna* refers to something that shows up for you just as you need it. It's a solution to a material need, like an answered prayer. It also refers to a form of spiritual nourishment. Manna keeps you going.

The origins of this concept go back to the story about the special bread that appeared every day to the Israelites as they wandered in the desert after they fled Egypt, where they had been slaves of the Pharaoh. Manna was their sustenance.

You don't need to be familiar with this story, which was written circa 1500 BCE. I'm going to share everything you need to know.

A *manna mindset* is an approach to our personal liberation and well-being that employs psychological and spiritual principles. It involves tapping into the power of our thoughts and taming our negative mental habits. It opens us to gratitude. It is characterized by positive expectancy, which creates the stepping-stones to an elevated consciousness. In turn, our elevated consciousness can change our reality and our circumstances.

Our goal is to create a state of elevated consciousness and remain there.

When you make the manna paradigm shift, providence emerges in every area of your life, from your finances and health to your work and relationships.

When you make the manna paradigm shift, you will gain the true power of choice. You will remember what it feels like to be free. You'll learn to shift your fearful thoughts. You will see that fear is a strawman that's easily knocked down rather than a real obstacle. You'll begin to follow the Universe as it guides you towards undreamed-of opportunities.

The teachings I will share with you in this book will help you escape any kind of mental entrapment you feel is limiting you from living your best life.

Terminology and Invitation

Throughout this book, I will use the word *Universe* interchangeably with the terms *Source, God, the Divine,* and the *Divine Mind.* These words and phrases refer to a higher level of consciousness that we can tap. Some people with spiritual inclinations might view this consciousness as spiritual energy. Physicists might view it as the unified (or quantum) field. I see it as both. Use whatever terminology makes sense to you.

And now, I invite you to learn the concepts and embrace the practices of *The Manna Paradigm Shift*— opening yourself to a more fulfilling life.

PART ONE

THE PRINCIPLES OF THE MANNA PARADIGM SHIFT

ONE

∞

A NEW PARADIGM OF LIVING

What if this was the moment your life changed?

During their flight from Egypt, manna was the bread that God gave the Hebrews every morning before sunrise. You may have heard this story in church or at temple when you were a kid or heard some cultural allusion to the notion of manna from heaven.

Manna was a miracle.

If not for this bread, these homeless people wandering through the wilderness would have starved. Every person was given an amount of manna depending on their appetite and need. However, the bread would not keep. It would rot by the next day, so it had to be eaten on arrival. Hoarding it was useless. The Hebrews had to rely on fresh manna every day. They had to trust.

The manna paradigm shift is so named because the solution to our material needs is the spiritual nourishment that keeps us going.

By Man or by Manna

When we endow humans and human institutions with power over us, we are making those people and institutions our "gods," and limiting ourselves and our possibilities. It is crippling to choose limited human nature over unlimited consciousness. We prevent ourselves from connecting with the Divine Mind within us. This is an inherent aspect of each of our beings.

To make the manna paradigm shift doesn't require you to adhere to a particular religion or any religion at all. You don't have to go to church or temple or even believe in a god. What is required is that you tap the energy of the Universe. If you can do this, you can make the manna paradigm shift.

"We are going to emancipate ourselves from mental slavery because whilst others might free the body, none but ourselves can free the mind. Mind is your only ruler, sovereign. The man who is not able to develop and use his mind is bound to be the slave of the other man who uses his mind, because man is related to man under all circumstances for good or ill."[1]

—Marcus Garvey

To Make the Manna Paradigm Shift

There are three steps to make the manna paradigm shift.

Step 1. Choose freedom. When you practice the manna mindset principles, you'll see how to choose freedom and the value in choosing freedom every moment. You'll learn how to liberate and support yourself.

Step 2. Turn away from your mental subjugation. Our thoughts have been conditioned by society. We've been conditioned not to believe in ourselves. We're conditioned to believe that our power comes from outside ourselves. Like obedient full-grown circus elephants that were conditioned as babies by trainers who placed a chain around one leg, we grow into adulthood unaware that we now have the strength to break the old chains that bind us. We don't realize we have the power to free ourselves.

Tune in to your intuition and turn away from the conditioned beliefs that hold you down. Don't let human laws be your ultimate authority on anything.

This doesn't mean to harm others or act recklessly. It means to question authority. Let no one be your mental master.

Abandon the it's-always-been-that-way mentality. In other words, just because something has "always" been done a certain way doesn't mean it can't be done differently now. Those were the same types of arguments used to keep segregation and other forms of oppression in place a mere few decades ago. As a culture, we no longer share our forebearers' beliefs on these and many other issues, including gay marriage and the right of women to vote and secure credit from banks in their own names.

To release yourself from mental subjugation, turn away from common beliefs, trends, and societal and familial expectations. Ignore them. Just because there was a recession in 2009 and 2020 doesn't mean that everyone experienced a financial downturn. Many people flourished. You have to turn away from the daily fearmongering and the voices that exist to keep you from making change or taking risks or pursuing your dreams.

Step 3. Connect with a source greater than your small self. Our power comes through our alignment with our Source. When you see yourself as separate from your Source, you feel isolated. However, when you tap into Source and its infinite potential you align with its creative power. By *Source,* I mean the life force that moves through you and everything else living on our planet. I mean God in its creative aspect.

This may be the hardest of the three principles to comprehend if you haven't had a spiritual experience or do not have religious faith. This will be an esoteric, ephemeral concept, until you've had a tangible experience of the unified field at work in your life or a demonstration of the power of a higher power. When you've felt the embodiment of a palpable presence, the peace that surpasses human understanding, or the feeling of divine love moving through your body, you remember on a cellular level that there is something greater, something infinitely more powerful than human consciousness alone, even after the sensation fades.

When we connect with the Higher Mind of the Universe, we are engaging with a consciousness with infinite capacity compared to our individual, finite minds. Aligning with this higher consciousness rather than our everyday, limited consciousness and physical senses is the key to our freedom.

As you adhere to the three fundamentals of the manna paradigm shift and follow the steps to create a manna mindset your liberation will begin.

TWO

⌒⌒

AN ANCIENT STORY OF LIBERATION

Tyranny over our minds is a form of subjugation.

Let me tell you an ancient story about liberation and the pursuit of freedom that is still relevant today. If you've ever been to a Passover seder, you may be familiar with the first part of the story.

The Hebrews were slaves in ancient Egypt and longed to be free of Pharaoh, the god king of Egypt. He ruled the people and was seen as an intercessor between the gods and man. To these people, Pharaoh was a tyrant. But despite his social status, Pharaoh feared they were becoming too powerful.

After hearing a prophecy that a baby boy would grow up and challenge him, Pharaoh put out a decree that all male Hebrew newborns be killed. This set certain events in motion. One mother ignored the laws of mankind (Pharaoh's decree) and put her faith in the Divine. To protect her son, Moses, from the death squads, she placed him in a small boat by the riverbank. She envisioned him as being safe, surrounded, and protected by the power of love and gave him to the river.

She let him go.

Pharaoh's daughter found baby Moses and adopted him into the royal family. Moses was raised as an Egyptian prince. Years later, he saw a slave-master beating a Hebrew slave and he killed the master. Branded a murderer, Moses fled to the desert where, as the story goes, God appeared as a burning bush. God introduced himself to Moses under the name "I AM that I AM" and told Moses that he needed to return to Egypt, and he would help him free the Hebrews from subjugation.

Moses returned to Egypt and demanded of Pharaoh, "Let my people go."

Pharaoh refused.

However, after God smote Egypt with a series of ten plagues, Pharaoh told the Hebrews to get out. They left in a hurry before their bread could rise. That's why Matzah, unleavened bread, is eaten on Passover. It marks the historic journey from slavery to freedom, from bondage to liberation.

We call this journey the Exodus.

The story of the Exodus has echoed as a symbol of freedom throughout history.

The motif has been embraced by early American settlers fleeing Europe, enslaved African Americans, and marginalized groups seeking civil rights in the 20th and 21st centuries. From LGBTQ people pursuing civil marriage rights and immigrants soliciting asylum, to women wanting full participation in the workplace and politics, the Exodus has symbolized freedom from man's tyranny over man.

Thomas Jefferson and Ben Franklin considered using Exodus imagery for the Great Seal of the United States, and Jefferson embraced the motto, "I have sworn upon the altar of god eternal hostility against every form of tyranny over *the mind of man*."[1]

Leaving Egypt and Freeing Ourselves from the Forms of Tyranny Over Our Minds

Metaphysics looks at the nature of consciousness and includes our perception, our awareness of our existence, and how we experience reality.

The Exodus story has a powerful metaphysical message about freedom that's just as relevant for us today as it was in antiquity, which has to do with our perception of our own freedom. The story is encoded with deeper meaning that can help us understand the inner workings of our minds and how our beliefs limit us. For example, the Hebrew word for Egypt is *Mitzrayim*, which means "narrow place" or "blockage."[2] Leaving Egypt, on the metaphysical level, means freeing ourselves from different forms of tyranny over our minds.

Egypt refers to restricted thinking. To narrow points of view and rigid beliefs. *Leaving Egypt* therefore is an allegory that tells us that we must free ourselves from subjugation first by our minds. The Exodus story reminds us that we have to leave our limited thinking behind to be free.

In this book, I will show you how to shift your consciousness and use your mind more effectively, so that you may experience the freedom, joy, and abundance you long for.

The Power of Thought

Erwin Schrödinger, the Noble Prize-winning quantum physicist who invented wave theory, said, "Every man's world picture is and always remains a construct of his mind and cannot be proved to have any other existence."[3] What this means is that our thoughts have the power to shape aspects of our reality.

Our thoughts are like seeds. They may seem small and inconsequential until we start to pay attention to them and energetically water them with our emotions. If we think a thought and feel it for a period of time, we give birth to its actual creation. The seed becomes the plant the longer we immerse ourselves in it.

The soil is where our individual minds meets the Divine Mind.

As we think a thought, we plant it in the soil. The soil provides our consciousness with the power to create. The plant is the out-picturing of our thoughts.

We plant seed-thoughts of health, prosperity, and happiness, and other things we want. We enjoy it when those thoughts manifest and our daily reality is filled with the tangible qualities of well-being, abundance, and joy.

Not All Plants Bear Fruit

Not every thought we have is going to bear fruit the way we would like it to. Just because we think a thought like, "I want a million dollars, a yellow Corvette, and my own private island," doesn't mean we're going to manifest those things.

Not All Plants Are Wanted

There are some seeds we don't want to grow. We can call negative thoughts that create things we do not want *weeds*. This phenomenon is where we get sayings like "Worrying is praying for what you don't want." Weeds can keep the good seeds from getting the nourishment they need. We need to be mindful of the thoughts we plant.

Some thoughts empower us, while others keep us tethered to unloving and destructive realities. Some thoughts create feelings and beliefs that keep us from leaving abusive or toxic relationships, for example, or shackle us to unsatisfying jobs, pursuing our callings, or even taking trips.

Our minds are plagued by all the reasons we believe we can't make a change. We often stay in situations that are bad for us because we think we can't do any better.

If we leave *this* relationship we may never find love again. We might not be able to make the mortgage payment or find a good apartment.

This roommate is bad, but the next roommate might be worse.

The next job might not pay as much. It might not have good health insurance and we could get sick.

If we quit our day job, we may still fail at our dream.

Thoughts like these keep us stuck and limited. They loop through our heads like rollercoasters with their predictable ups and downs.

When we're stuck in limited thinking, we find it impossible to trust life. We treat our bosses as if they're demigods. We make our bank accounts the validation of our self-worth. Our consciousness is limited by these habitual patterns of thinking.

Making changes in our way of thinking and getting unstuck from scenarios in our lives that are limited is what I will refer to as *leaving Egypt*. We must leave Egypt if we want to be free.

Do any of the dilemmas I've just described sound familiar to you? Do you find yourself afraid to make a change and to leave something behind? You're not alone.

The games we played as kids, like musical chairs, are deeply ingrained in our psyches. If we give up our spot and don't quickly get our butt in that next seat before another person, we're out of the game. Games of scarcity such as this one made an indelible impression on our innocent young minds. We didn't realize we could just say "screw this game" and go create our own. Find another option. That's what leaving Egypt is about.

Yes, my friend, you have a choice. You can leave Egypt and make the manna paradigm shift.

What's Your Egypt? Self-Reflection

Where do you feel stuck or trapped in your life?
Do you feel impotent when confronted by your Pharaohs?

Dr. Eileen J. Kenny, D.C.

Oil of Oregano –
1, 2x a day
until bottle is empty

L-Threonine – 2 in Am
10 minutes before food

DAVINA KOTULSKI

(626) 398 0292
1911 North Lake Ave., Altadena, CA 91001

THREE

∾

CHOOSE FREEDOM

The first step in freedom is choosing it.

The first step in making a manna paradigm shift is to claim freedom for ourselves. In order to choose freedom for ourselves, we must be willing to believe that something more is possible, even if we don't know how it will be possible yet. This turns our focus away from our mental entrapment and creates a sense of hope and personal agency.

Take a moment to write down the answer to these questions.

Where do you feel stuck or trapped in your life? Your relationship? Your job? Something else?

What changes do you want to make in your life?

In order to choose freedom, we need clarity on how and where we're giving away our power. *Who or what are you giving your power to—which people, places, and things?*

Where and when are you giving your power away? In what situations?

Sometimes before we can choose something new we have to let go of something. *What do you need to let go of?*

What do you need to turn away from so you can live the life you desire?

While we can't predict how our lives will turn out, having a vision can be helpful. *What would choosing freedom look like for you?*

What would create more joy and satisfaction in your life?

If you could choose something new, what would you choose for yourself?

You may find yourself avoiding answering these questions because you're afraid of what will come up if you do. You are likely afraid of changing. Sometimes we fear that if we face the truth about the people or situations in our lives, those people might leave or reject us, or that a situation will change.

Even more frightening, we ourselves may want to leave a relationship or situation, and the thought of taking action and initiating changes feels daunting.

Just remember this, by skipping the questions and avoiding having a heart to heart with yourself, you remain in mental chains.

The Clock Is Ticking

Akiko, a successful accountant and mother of twins, wanted the freedom to spend more time with her children. She took time off after their birth, but within three months, she was back at her demanding job. Being away from her twins caused Akiko emotional turmoil. She knew she was missing pivotal moments in their early development and the ability to make a significant impact on their lives.

As a mid-level manager, Akiko brought in a six-figure salary and had a good position within her company, one with great perks and retirement potential. While Akiko excelled at her job, she didn't particularly like it, and it required a lot of her attention. She was tired after returning home from work and cranky as she prepared dinner. Akiko had little attention to give her children over mealtime, and once the twins were bathed and in bed, she found herself rushing through story time so she could pour herself a glass of wine and crash on the couch. This was not how she envisioned motherhood.

Akiko negotiated working from home a few days a week and began work early those mornings to get more done while the twins slept. She spread out her vacation days, taking afternoons off here and there to be home earlier with the twins. It still wasn't enough.

As the years ticked by, Akiko kept trying to figure out how to take a year off to be with her children. When she came to see me she'd already saved up a year's worth of living expenses. She told me she'd wished she'd quit her job a year ago or requested a leave of absence so she could take the twins out of daycare. She spoke fondly of how she longed to spend a year with them having adventures, teaching them, cooking with them, playing with them. It was how some of my clients speak about their dreams to travel the world. It was clear that having twelve months off to spend with her children was Akiko's most important dream.

But the clock was ticking.

Despite her savings, Akiko was terrified to take an action. She was paralyzed by the fear that her dream of taking a year off would screw up her financial foundation. Over the nine months of our working together, Akiko kept trying to "get her ducks in a row." She kept anticipating what could go wrong. "I get one thing handled and then something else comes up," she said, exasperated. She regularly repeated, "I wish I'd taken last year off before I had this extra expense." Or "I wish I'd taken a leave before we needed to think about where the twins' were going to go to elementary school. Hindsight is 20/20."

I empathized with Akiko's conundrum, with her fears. I remembered how scary it was to make my own leap of faith. I could only imagine how much scarier it would be with the fear of not being able to provide for your children. At the same time, I saw Akiko's desire to take time off to be with her kids as an even more compelling reason for her to make the manna paradigm shift. It was not only her own precious life at stake. She needed to make a real investment of time, energy, and focus in her children's lives—she was losing time that she could never get back with them. They were growing. They were never going to be four, five, or six again. They were going to be required to go to school soon and the opportunity to have the luxury of lazy days with them would be gone forever.

After several months of circling the decision to make her exodus, Akiko abruptly ended coaching. She'd gotten too busy at work. Frankly, I think she was tired of climbing up the diving board and not jumping off. It was just easier to stop. She wasn't willing or able to choose freedom for herself. Her fear had a tenacious grip over her.

Five months later, I received a call from Akiko. We met for a session. She was visibly anxious. "I'm up for a promotion. I don't want it. I want to resign or take a leave of absence. But I don't want to burn any bridges. I wish I'd said something months ago," she said, repeating her favorite refrain. "Hindsight is 20/20."

"The Universe has been encouraging you to take a leap of faith for a long time." I wanted to say. I didn't. I just listened.

Akiko had shared that since our previous sessions she'd started meditating daily and had stopped drinking completely. She had made herself more receptive and was listening more deeply to her higher self.

"I'm missing those cherished moments with the twins," she said. "I don't know what I'm going to do for work if I quit."

Even though much of what Akiko was saying was familiar, she was different. This time she meant business. I could feel her heart was fully in it. She said she was ready to choose freedom. She was ready to make the manna paradigm shift.

For the first time, she shared with me that her dad had died of a heart attack at his job because he was a workaholic. She didn't want that for herself. She realized she was teaching the twins that life was about working until you die. We explored how children seeing their parents empowered, rather than in servitude, especially in unhappy jobs, helps them feel empowered to make excellent choices, not just settle.

Akiko wanted to break the cycle but was afraid we were heading into another recession. I shared with her that I had been in graduate school during the 1992 recession and had no memory of it whatsoever. Akiko remembered that she had graduated college during the 2008 recession and couldn't get a job.

"How did you deal with that?" I asked.

"I decided to go to London for a year and teach financial management."

"That sounds amazing," I said. "How brave and resilient of you and what a creative way to respond to those circumstances."

She smiled the biggest smile I'd ever seen. "It was the best decision I ever made."

I asked her to get in touch with the resilient energy that she had back then. "What does your heart want?" I asked.

"I want to ask my boss for nine months off starting January first with the option to come back part time," she said.

It was the most concrete and clear she'd ever been in all of our time working together.

After our session, Akiko declined the promotion. She told her boss she wanted to take a one-year sabbatical and return to work part-time. Her boss agreed. Akiko chose freedom. After that, she had the time she wanted with her twins.

The clock wasn't just ticking for Akiko, of course. It's ticking for all of us. We only have a certain amount of time on our planet.

If you're in your twenties, you may feel as if you have the luxury of time or you may feel a sense of urgency to get out there and prove yourself.

Around the age of thirty, if you haven't accomplished important goals in your life you may start to feel anxious and even panicked about using your time meaningfully.

Around the age of thirty-five, the beginning of a stage of life that some people would call the second act, if you've climbed the first couple of rungs on the ladder of success and achieved a few early societal milestones, such as getting married and having kids, you may start to ask yourself, *Is this all there is?*

Around the age of forty, if you haven't made changes to your scenario, you may find yourself beginning to seriously reassess your life. As if some unseen evolutionary force is at play like the one that impels the caterpillar to begin to spin its chrysalis for transformation, the Universe may even give you a nudge.

In mid-life we begin to feel our mortality, maybe subtly at first, and then more acutely. The volume gets turned up so that every area of our lives in which we are dissatisfied becomes more discordant. We start questioning: Are we making the right choices? Are we where we want to be? Is this the right marriage? The right job? Is there such a thing even as the right anything? Most importantly, are we doing what we came here to do? Are we being who we came here to be? Are we playing small and staying stuck because we are afraid? Where are we keeping life from flowing through us?

In the third act of your life, which might begin in your mid-fifties or even later, since you don't know how long you have remaining, the tension to truly live your life and be free is even more pronounced. Yet it's also a time when you're dealing with the Pharaohs like ageism and your survival fears. Will you be denied a job because of your age? Are you no longer relevant? Will you be overlooked? Are you out of style? Not up on the most recent tech? Will your money run out? Will you get sick and not be able to afford care?

These are deep existential questions. We can turn and run from them or we can face them.

No matter what our age, we will feel best when we invest our time wisely in what we care about be that education, relationships, spirituality, travel, creativity, life or career.

Freedom of Choice and Making the Choice to Be Free

How we choose freedom for ourselves will vary between individuals.

For Tania, it meant quitting her job at a high-tech company with twelve-hour workdays and finding a job closer to her home. It was hard for her to let go of a position she had worked so hard to achieve. Making a change that appeared to place her on a lower rung of the achievement ladder made her doubt her worth. Through our work together, Tania began to see corporate ladder-climbing was designed to prioritize work over work/life balance, physical and emotional well-being, and family connection. It was created by employers as an incentive to get employees to play by their rules and had nothing to do with exploring or celebrating her inherent worth.

Two months after leaving the tech job, Tania said she felt better about herself. She had lost twenty-five pounds because now she had time to plan her meals and was no longer eating fast-food in the car and stress eating at work. She felt good about her body and even started dating again. She shared that even though she was making less money at her new job, she was spending significantly less money on gas and was glad to not be putting additional wear and tear on her car. When Tania chose freedom for herself her whole life began to shift.

During the pandemic, I worked with Max, a 20-something software engineer. He choose freedom by correcting his work/life balance. Since he no longer had to make the insane three-hour commute to his 10-hour-per-day tech job, Max chose to use the extra time to engage in daily exercise and to make healthy home-cooked meals. As a result, he lost 50 pounds in six months. His outlook on life improved and so did his self-esteem.

For my client Peter, it meant ending his marriage with a woman who thought his dreams and desires were foolish. Though Peter was a good provider and loving father to his children, he lived with his wife's constant ridicule and derision when he had an idea or wanted to pursue one of his passion projects. When he stopped focusing on his fears and trusted that there would be enough resources for him and the children, he ended his marriage.

Sometimes choosing freedom means creating space to do the things we love.

Arnie turned down a promotion at the bank so he could spend more time with his family and teach improv and acting classes.

Carla told her teenagers that they would need to be responsible for cooking a meal for themselves two nights a week, so she would have time to exercise.

Choosing freedom might include investing in ourselves.

Kevin's freedom came in the form of buying a café where he and his wife could work together and have a bigger part in raising their kids.

Shireen bought a chiropractic business so that she could be her own boss.

Kris had always dreamt of going to art school. So, they took money out of their 401K to pay for it.

Choosing freedom might mean speaking our truth to loved ones rather than simply going along with their expectations for us or our behavior.

Lily told her husband that she wanted to hire a part-time nanny so she could go back to work.

Yasmin's liberation was telling her family that she was going to marry the man she loved—and telling the man she loved she was not going to put up with any more of his jealousy if she was going to be his wife.

Sometimes choosing freedom means coming to terms with our biggest fears and choosing to face them head on. This was the case for my friend Faleen. For her, choosing freedom meant leaving her abusive husband after she was diagnosed with stage 4 cancer and dying peacefully in an apartment that overlooked the ocean.

For my client Sarita, it meant coming to terms with the age discrimination she was experiencing in the job market. Rather than continue to be turned down for jobs that she was highly qualified for, Sarita started her own home healthcare business and took control of her destiny.

For Isabelle, one of my webinar participants in her third act, choosing freedom meant facing financial fears by taking on fewer financial consulting contracts, so she could instead start the interior decorating business that had been her lifelong dream job. It was a huge leap of faith for her financially to initiate a new career path. As soon as she chose to make the leap, she saw immediate positive results in both of her businesses.

How you choose freedom will be individual to you.

The important thing is that you make a personal choice that sets you free. You choose a new story for yourself. You choose to take your power back from whatever outside sources you're giving your power away to: a relationship, your kids, your boss, your parents, the economy, the job market, the media, the government, perfectionism, fear of rejection, guilt, and so on. Stop bestowing people, institutions, and social contracts and constructs with godlike power over you and instead decide to create your new reality. You don't have to know how it will work. Your only job is to choose something new. That's your first step.

By choosing something new, you're planting the seed of a new reality in your subconscious. You've moved in the direction of freedom. Congratulations!

FOUR

BREAK YOUR MENTAL CHAINS

Our fears bind us, while our faith frees us.

In order to make the manna paradigm shift, we must break our mental chains. The strongest mental chain is fear. Fear causes worst case-scenario thinking and rumination. When fear takes over our minds, we become paralyzed. Fear keeps us from acting.

We dwell on what could go wrong. We watch the news and regurgitate the bad stuff occurring around the globe. We look for proof of our failure or the failure of others. We tell ourselves negative things under the pretense of safety. We come by this thinking naturally, due to the negativity bias.

The Negativity Bias

Psychological researchers have identified a phenomenon whereby people tend to place more value on the negative aspects of an experience than on its positive aspects.[1] This is called the *negativity bias*.

Negativity bias may also contribute to *negativity dominance,* which is where we label an event negatively even when it has positive aspects.

The negativity bias may be directly related to our survival instincts. For example, we don't go back to our favorite sushi restaurant because we remember the one time the sushi made us sick and forget the hundred other times we ate there without incident. Because of our tendency to remember the negative more than the positive aspects of experience, memories of the positive don't remain with us as long as the negative.[2]

This is a contributing factor to why we feel afraid to make changes. The fear of failure and other survival fears carry more weight psychologically in our minds than the possibility of success when we consider trying new things.

Referring back to the allegory of the Exodus, on the psychological level *Egypt* is a metaphor for the negativity-biased mental state where fears and cognitive distortions dominate. That's why you can't break your chains until you're aware of what they are and how they are impacting you.

Fear Creates Distortion

Fears can turn into cognitive distortions: fear thoughts that have spun out of control. We must identify these fears because they negatively impact us in myriad ways, including making us unhappy in our relationships, judging ourselves and others in a poor light, and expecting the worst.

According to Stanford psychiatrist David Burns, author of *The Feeling Good Handbook,* cognitive distortions include overgeneralization, focusing on the negative, disqualifying the positive, predicting the future, emotional reasoning, all-or-nothing thinking, personalization, should statements, catastrophizing, labeling, and attempts at mind reading.[3] These distortions are our mental chains. They limit us. They are negative in nature and keep us from acting. These distortions are negative appraisals of ourselves, others, or our circumstances.

Cognitive distortions most typically are *over-generalizations,* thoughts that take a shred of evidence and make erroneous conclusions—and usually to our detriment. This is where we take one negative experience and apply it to every aspect of something. An event is interpreted in terms of "never" and "always." For example, "That person didn't want to date me. This always happens to me. I'm never going to get a date." "Donna didn't invite me to the party. I'm always alienating people."

Most of these cognitive distortions are self-evident, such as *focusing on the negative,* where we notice what's not working, or *disqualifying the positive,* where we ignore what is going well, what is possible, what is good. In our heads, it sounds something like this: "Sure, I might have had some success in the past, but that was just dumb luck. I failed this time to get the client/contract/ job/relationship I wanted."

Predicting the future means we imagine worst-case scenarios, how things won't work out, how we will fail. It sounds like: "If I leave my marriage, I will never have another romantic relationship."

Catastrophizing is taking it to the ultimate extreme. "I will be alone for the rest of my life." "If I quit this job. No one will hire me, and I'll end up homeless."

All-or-nothing thinking causes us to see extremes and act in extremes. You might recognize this from the children in your lives. it sounds like: "If I can't have ice cream I don't want any dessert!" "If I don't get this publishing contract I will never write again." "If I don't sell a painting by June it means I'm a talentless hack."

Labeling is insulting yourself. "I'm a freak." "I'm half a person." "I'm an old maid."

Personalization is when you attribute someone else's behavior to yourself, when in fact their behavior may have to do with their own internal or external realities that have nothing to do with you. "People don't say 'hi' to me because they don't want to be around me." "Susan didn't ask me how my day was going because she finds me dreadfully boring."

Mind reading involves interpreting others' behaviors without asking them. "My girlfriend is ignoring me because she wants to break up with me." "Philip didn't respond to my text about the job because he doesn't think I should apply."

Cognitive distortions leave us feeling disempowered. They are the opposite of empowering thoughts and they keep us stuck in self-doubt and too fearful to take an action in our lives that would free us from unpleasant circumstances. But we must take an action if we are going to free ourselves, even if that action is simply pivoting our thoughts.

Some cognitive distortions arise from experiences of abuse. Those who were verbally abused as children and told that they were "stupid" or "not good enough" or "never going to amount to anything" may have internalized those statements and then repeat those negative thoughts in their everyday lives or when they find themselves in challenging or novel situations.

Negative Thoughts Create Negative Feelings

When a negative thought takes root in our minds, it creates a corresponding emotional and physical reaction in our body. When we feel the impact of that thought, it becomes embodied. We are hosting it. Our bodies and our body chemistry become the soil to grow that weed and give it the ability to affect our lives.

For example, if you think about your partner/spouse cheating on you, even if it's never happened, you'll feel angry. You might even feel sick to your stomach. The thoughts of this alone create sensations in your body. You may start to create a whole reality, even if it's a delusional one, around your thoughts.

Perhaps you're familiar with Shakespeare's character Othello, who believes his wife is unfaithful to him. Told lies to this effect by a malicious subordinate, Othello becomes besieged by thoughts of her infidelity, and he ends up murdering her and killing himself.

Thoughts Are Powerful

While engaged in a ten-day, silent vipassanā meditation retreat. I imagined something horrible happening to my spouse while I was away and incommunicado. After having the intrusive thought, I was unable to quiet my mind or rid myself of the dread it conjured. The repugnant thought caused a sickening feeling to rise inside me. Nothing had happened. It was only a thought. However, that thought had the power to disrupt my mental and physical equilibrium.

I began to panic, and I could not find relief.

At the end of the meditation session, I went to the teacher's assistant and briefly broke silence, requesting that they contact my spouse and confirm that she was okay. At that moment, I was under the influence of the cognitive distortion called *emotional reasoning*, believing that my thought and subsequent fear reaction were evidence of some real event.

To be clear, this was not an intuition. Intuition is different. This was purely a fear-based thought that arose in my mind as I was engaged in a practice of quieting it. But this thought was so impactful that I was unable to calm myself or continue my meditation retreat without asking the staff to please check on her for me.

Of course, my spouse was fine. And, as the ten-hour days of meditation continued, I saw how the mind—especially my mind—worked, how it created fear-based thoughts. I observed the familiar thought patterns my mind frequented and the landscapes of the subjects it traversed.

We can use our thoughts for good or for evil. We can think thoughts that create more good feelings in our bodies and experiences in our lives, or we can think thoughts that create negative chemistry in our bodies and ultimately lead to more negative experiences.

Thought Stopping

On the psychological level, to leave Egypt requires us to do some serious thought stopping and thought pivoting. Every time a thought about lack, limitation, failure, or negativity shows up, we need to stop it. We should do our best not to let it take root in our minds.

Since most things don't turn out to be worst-case scenarios, intentional thought stopping helps us calm down and stay focused on the here and now. We may face some difficult challenges and need to deal with some heavy things, but all we ever really have to do is deal with one moment of our lives and thoughts at a time.

When a negative thought comes up take a deep breath.

Ask yourself:
Is this thought true?
If this thought is not true-what else might be true?
Is this thought a cognitive error? Which one?
If it were true how would I handle it?

For example, Philip didn't respond to my text because he doesn't think I should apply for the job.

Is this thought true? Not necessarily.

If this thought is not true-what else might be true? Philip might be busy working on his projects. Philip is someone who speaks his mind. He would tell me if he thought I shouldn't apply for the job.

Is this thought a cognitive error? Which one? Yes, mind-reading.

If it were true how would I handle it? I'd decide if I still wanted to apply for the job.

By asking ourselves if a thought is true we can begin to engage reason. If it's not true, we can ask ourselves if we are under the influence of cognitive distortion and examine which possible thinking error we are committing. This redirects us.

Break Your Chains

Take several minutes to answer the following questions. Writing down your responses will be even more revealing than simple reflection as it helps us to be concrete.

Before you begin, you may want to review your answers to the questions at the end of the last chapter regarding the things in your life you want to change.

Why haven't you made the change yet? In other words, what thoughts (if any) are keeping you stuck?

What thinking errors do you make the most?

What are some thoughts you have that limit you?

Where do you give up before you even start?

What (if anything) have you been making your ultimate authority?

What (if any) are the narrow places in your mind or in what areas is your thinking constricted?

What are your survival thoughts?

What are some exceptions to these limiting beliefs?

What comes up for you as you answer these questions? Do you see any places where you're giving away your power? Do you see what's stopping you? Are your fears strawmen, false ideas and propositions?

FIVE

꩜

CONNECT WITH THE HIGHER MIND

Aligning with the Higher Mind is the key to freedom.

I believe that our power comes to us, through our alignment with our Source. Your true self is your connection to that source energy. When you tap into Source and its infinite potential you are aligned with its creative power. When you connect with the Higher Mind (the intelligence that runs the Universe), you are engaging an elevated consciousness, one with infinite capacity compared to your finite personal mind. Aligning with this higher consciousness rather than your everyday consciousness as a human being and the information provided to you by your limited physical senses, is your key to freedom.

This is manna consciousness.

Manna Consciousness

Manna consciousness trusts that everything we need will show up when we need it. It is characterized by the sort of faith described in the Bible (Hebrews 11:1): "Now faith is the substance of things hoped for, the evidence of things not seen."[1] In manna consciousness, we turn from fear and trust the Universe. We're more relaxed and open because we are anchored into a state of positive expectancy and gratitude. Manna consciousness is an extension of the mindset we've previously discussed that knows that our needs will be provided for, beyond mere survival. Through manna consciousness, we influence, even create, our circumstances and realities.

Manna consciousness focuses on the positive attributes of experience. When we feel gratitude and appreciation and have trust in ourselves, others, and the world, we are connecting with its elevated consciousness. For some people this comes easily. Like a singer who can sing high notes without struggling, some people can easily adjust their mindset to a higher vibration. For others, it requires practiced steps to cultivate manna consciousness. The easiest way to elevate the vibration of your consciousness is through an intentional focus on positive thinking and appreciation.

Through the teachings that follow, you will become like a singer who practices scales and can rise from lower notes to higher notes. You will learn how to ascend your mind to a higher vibration so you can anchor into the higher notes of elevated consciousness. The notes are always there, but you only experience them when you are able to reach them.

You'll See It When You Believe It

When you allow yourself to suspend negative judgment and fix your mind on positive expectancy and engage in practices that elevate your mind's vibrational frequency, as will be discussed specifically in chapter 9, you will begin to experience manna consciousness.

I know it sounds like magic. You have to be open to experiencing it to see it. It's like one of those 3D optical illusion posters. You can't see the hidden image at first, it just looks like chaos. However, once you see the hidden image, you can't unsee it, and now you know that it's possible for something to exist that at first you don't see.

It must have been incredible the first time a scientist looked through the lens of a microscope and saw the tiny amoebas in a drop of water that aren't available to the naked eye. Or when an astronomer first looked through a telescope and saw the pockmarked surface of the moon with its craters.

It didn't mean the molecules or craters weren't there a minute before. They were there, the scientists just couldn't see them until they had access to the right tools.

After viewing our planet from space, NASA astronaut and U.S. naval officer and aeronautical engineer Edgar Mitchell commented that he became aware of a continuum of human perception. He said, "At one end is material consciousness. At the other end is what we call 'field consciousness' where a person is at one with the Universe. Just by looking at our planet on the way back,

I felt a field consciousness state" —meaning, he felt the unity and oneness of all life on the planet as well as being connected to the entire Universe.[2]

Just like Mitchell experienced the world differently when he connected with the higher consciousness he calls field consciousness, when you anchor into manna consciousness, your perspective will change. You will see and experience the world differently.

The Miracle of Manna

Manna is not a piece of bread. It's a promise that when we shift our consciousness and connect our thoughts to the Higher Mind what we need will be provided to us. We always have access to the Higher Mind. Whether we fight against this concept or are open to embracing it, it is always there for us.

In order to receive this promise, you must first see it in your mind and feel it in your body. You must be the embodiment of what you wish to create.

To embody manna consciousness, we begin by setting our minds in the here and now, which means in the "I am" as opposed to in the "will do," the "will be," or the "is not."

I *am* is the present tense of the verb "to be" from the perspective of the person who is speaking. No matter our current circumstances, if we can shift our consciousness and embody the I AM of any situation we've initiated a new chain of events, a new reality for ourselves. Notice the difference in the power of saying, "I AM healthy," NOT "I will be healthy," or "I am not healthy."

I AM is a divine phrase. It is what God said to Moses on the mountain. "I Am that I AM." When we say these words to ourselves or anyone else, we gain access to our divine power.

I AM is the only state of manna consciousness and the present is the only time zone in which the promise of manna can be fulfilled.

Even if you're going through a health crisis, you want to affirm "I AM healthy." I know this might be hard to do, especially if you're going through a health crisis, yet this is the energy you want to connect with. If that's not possible or it feels like a lie, then say something that feels true for you, like, "I am caring for my health, I am caring for my body, I am becoming healthy." This is a way to stay affirmative and in the present. We speak in affirmation of positive things because whatever we pay attention to magnifies.

Another example of an affirmation is, "I AM supported by the Universe," not "I will be supported" or "I'm not supported," or even the conditional idea, "I must do something to be supported by the Universe."

All other notions bring in doubt, only I AM is certain. We must embrace that certainty.

Your Mind on Manna and Manna on Your Mind

We can deepen our manna consciousness by the nature of our self-talk and keeping our minds trained on empowering thoughts like the statements below.

"I'm always in the right place at the right time."

"All my needs are met in perfect timing."

"The money comes at the right time."

"Good things always happen to me."

"Life supports me."

"I am surrounded by a loving presence and loving people gravitate to me."

"I am magnetic to my good."

"I always have more than enough."

"Everything always works out for me."

Sometimes we might have a contrary reaction to positive statements. We may find one particular phrase irksome or take issue with it. For example, we might bristle at the affirmation "Good things happen to me" because when we hear it we immediately think of all the bad things that have happened.

"Good things" and "bad things" are relative. Something that's bad for the ego might be good for the soul on occasion. Additionally, something we label as a bad thing might lead to something we would label as a good thing.

Sherman Alexie had congenital hydrocephalus as a kid. His medical condition resulted in his being excluded from sports, so he became an avid reader who excelled at academics. Alexie was accepted on scholarship to medical school at Gonzaga University but soon realized in dissection class that he was too squeamish to become a doctor. He dropped out of medical school and enrolled in a creative writing course at a state university. Was it unlucky that he had hydrocephalus or that he was squeamish in medical school or were these things both perfect because they led him to his eventually becoming a *New York Times* best-selling author?

Perhaps you can see that good and bad are relative, but you find yourself making the cognitive error of disqualifying the positive. Whatever you react most strongly to, this is the area that needs the most attention and healing for you. No two people react to the same things identically. Your reactions are information about your own thinking and focus.

What We Focus On, We Create

Making positive statements and focusing on the good keeps us in a mental state of positive expectancy in which we are available for more good things to happen— wide open to people and opportunities.

And when we engage in empowering thoughts and positive self-talk, we show up with an openness in our body language that is visible to others. People perceive us as confident and interact with us differently than when our body language communicates fear, anxiety, reserve, or desperation.

Confirmation bias is the interpretation of any new information as evidence of our existing beliefs or theories. If we perceive life and the world, among other things, in a negative way, then anything that happens to us fits into that schema. But . . . if we perceive life and the world, and so forth, in a positive way, then anything that happens to us will be viewed as part of our positive point of view.

The world is neither exclusively negative nor exclusively positive. There are experiences we may deem negative or positive, but the world is not against us. It doesn't favor us or disfavor us.

Just because life is negative and positive in equal measure, doesn't mean it stays balanced or neutral. How we think and the actions we take as a result shifts our experiences. You'll notice that if you focus on the negative, you'll feel bad about yourself and life. While if you choose to focus on the positive and cultivate a gratitude practice, you'll feel happier.

Similarly, the more optimistic you are the more life will turn in your favor. Research has found that people who are more optimistic are more likely to get a job and even get promoted.[3] Additionally, according to a study by the University of Warwick, positive, happy people are more productive.[4] The study found that happy people were 12 percent more productive and unhappy people were 10 percent less productive.

Shawn Achor, author of *The Happiness Advantage*, also found that happiness fuels success and work productivity, a phenomenon he called the *happiness advantage*. People who are happy perform better and have more success in business.[5]

Yes, I know there are exceptions. But belief and positive energy do have an impact. Tangible side effects of being in manna consciousness include a sense of inner peace, trusting life, following inner guidance, acting with joy and spontaneity, and feeling good about yourself and others. This doesn't preclude action. This is part of what it means when we say, "God helps those who help themselves."

For far too many of us our natural state is unhappiness. If we are ever to experience more agency over our lives, we need to elevate our consciousness. Gratitude, inner peace, appreciation, and joy are elevated states of consciousness. Our intention should be trained on creating/anchoring into an elevated state as frequently as possible.

Elevating Your Mind or Focusing Your Mind?

The Higher Mind and the promise of the manna it provides is always there for us. The challenge, however, is keeping our minds focused on images of what we want, rather than on images of what we don't want.

Our goal is to consistently hold a positive I AM frequency. Yet too frequently we hold the image of what we don't want in our minds and create from there. We doubt. We imagine ourselves failing. And this is counterproductive because what we focus on we create.

When we worry, when we doubt, it's as if we're inviting what we don't want. Therefore, we must focus our minds on what we want and keep our internal dialogue and external speech in line with our vision for what we want and good outcomes.

This is simple, but not easy, which is the reason we have to train our minds.

We can know that our job is to get a clear vision of what we wish to manifest in our life but keeping our attention there, without wavering, may seem impossible. We have to engage in regular mind-body activities that create the positive mental state that allows *manna* to flow to us. The 30-Day Manna Challenge (see chapter 16) was designed to support you in this.

Manna is a metaphor for the creative substance that begins to build our desired reality like jigsaw puzzle pieces coming together. Manna may show up in the form of new friends, opportunities, leads. Manna can be a hunch we get or an email invitation that leads to the next thing. Manna can be a chance meeting that gets you to take an action that you've been putting off. Manna can be an inspirational quote that boosts your confidence and puts a pep in your step on a hard day. Manna can be a coupon that arrives in the mail or a great sale on something you've needed.

Manna is not just one thing. It's whatever is needed in the present moment. Your task is to recognize manna as it appears in your life and give thanks for it. Take every opportunity to feed the positive consciousness that you are developing, and it will grow and grow and grow.

There's an old Cherokee story about the two wolves who live inside us battling for dominance. One wolf is good and the other is evil.

The evil wolf is filled with anger, envy, jealousy, sorrow, regret, greed, arrogance, self-pity, guilt, resentment, inferiority, lies, false pride, superiority, and ego.

The good wolf is filled with joy, peace, love, hope, serenity, humility, kindness, benevolence, empathy, generosity, truth, compassion and faith.

We each have a decision to make moment to moment. *Which wolf will we feed?*

My client Amanda, a seasoned real estate agent, found herself feeding the evil wolf. She knew her negative thoughts were blocking her manna consciousness. Amanda told me. "I think that when things don't come together, I feel like I'm lagging. I engage in thoughts that create more blockages. Then I waste my time and energy. I feel frustrated and struggle to stay on top of things. I find myself working 24/7 and things feel like a log jam. I feel like I'm pushing the river and paddling upstream. My frustration increases in intensity and I become very frustrated with myself. When I'm affirming flow in the Universe, energy pours to me and from me."

I encouraged Amanda to declare her last statement as an affirmation. "I know the energy of the Universe pours to me and through me."

Then I encouraged her to say what she wanted to happen. "I want the seller to choose my client."

"Great," I said. "However, how can you take that to a higher place? For example," I suggested, "'I want my buyer to find and buy a home that they love and is the best fit for them and for the sellers.' See how that's a bit different? It doesn't feel desperate."

I encouraged her to shift her focus from just benefitting herself to envisioning and inviting a situation that was the best for everyone. This sort of minor modification in our thinking reminds us we live in an interconnected Universe and that when we take our focus off of our scarcity and lack fears and look for the win-win for everyone we are engaging with a higher vibration.

Amanda got it.

"What else do you want?" I asked.

"I want my listing to sell this weekend. So, I'm going to shift that to 'I invite and trust the Universe to bring forward the perfect buyer for this home in perfect timing.'"

"You've got it," I replied.

"When I get the feeling of allowing the energy to flow through me, I feel energized and stimulated. I know this will attract people because of the energy I'm putting out."

"What does that energy feel like?" I asked.

"It's a calming energy, not a pressure."

"What other practices have you learned that will help you create that calming energy?" Amanda smiled. "Meditation, saying and embodying my affirmations, and visualizing."

"What will you visualize?"

Amanda shared that she would visualize herself in a variety of potential buyer and seller situations in which she was exuding calm and confidence.

Those visualizations were Amanda leaning into her manna consciousness, and as she began to imagine herself in these situations, Amanda relaxed. She was breathing more easily and smiling. Her humor had returned. The way she was now describing how she would approach her work was a distinctly different energy than how she had previously described it as "pushing the river" and "paddling upstream."

Amanda began to accept that certain things were out of her control. However, by doing the things that were in her control (meditation, affirmations, visualizations) she was anchoring into the manna mindset and she was able to shift how she felt inside and that was a far better emotional place for her to be. She knew she had put her best foot forward and then she was able to let it go. Now she was able to trust in the timing of things which allowed her to feel empowered, instead of overwhelmed. Even if it didn't work out how she wanted, she knew she did everything she could which put her in the highest possible mindset.

The Manna Mindset Manifesto:
Daily Affirmation

It's time for you to claim this new reality for yourself.
Use the Manna Mindset Manifesto below daily to
help yourself align with the Higher Mind. By stating it
aloud at least once a day, preferably in the morning, you
will connect with your own creative power and a power
greater than yourself.

*"I choose freedom. I am a sovereign being, free from
enslavement. I have a direct connection with the source of all
life. The Universe is my source and sufficiency in all things. All
of my needs are met by the Universe in perfect timing. I receive
manna from heaven daily and I am grateful."*

PART TWO

ര∿

LIVE FROM THE MANNA MINDSET

In Part One, we discussed the three steps that make up the manna paradigm shift.

The first step in making the manna paradigm shift was making a choice. Choosing your freedom, freedom from the past, freedom from oppressive forces in your life, freedom from limiting beliefs and reality. With this step, you chose a new reality for yourself.

The second step in the process was breaking free from your mental chains. Identifying your limiting thoughts, doubts, and thinking errors, the mental habits that kept you stuck and constricted. Then turning away from them, choosing to see those thoughts as false.

The third step was realizing there is universal consciousness, the Higher Mind.

Now, in Part Two, you'll focus on how to create the manna mindset using discrete practices that, taken together, will guide you to elevate your consciousness to connect with the Higher Mind in a state of manna consciousness.

Manna consciousness is something that always exists. Some of us may naturally dwell in that state or reach it easily because we don't have a lot of resistance to it. Some of us are already actively engaged in practices that connect us with manna consciousness, such as positive thinking, being appreciative, and expecting the best, among other things. Others of us need to begin these practices.

Imagine musical notes and singing. There are musical notes that are easily in our range and others that are harder for us to reach. High notes exist in reality whether or not our voices can sing those notes or not. If we want our voice to be able to hit those high notes we will need to practice scales that allow us to hit them. Kind of like building a ramp or climbing up a ladder to reach something that is out of our everyday reach.

Unlike musical notes where you are going to be limited by your vocal range, everyone can connect to their higher consciousness. You just need to keep practicing. When you practice these teachings, you will be able to create a manna mindset. And when you create a manna mindset, you will be able to anchor yourself in manna consciousness ongoingly.

The Nine Fundamental Elements of Creating the Manna Mindset

There are nine fundamental elements to creating a manna mindset so you can make the manna paradigm shift. Every chapter that follows covers one of these fundamentals. While I will try to parse them out to make them more obvious, you will notice that many are intertwined. Like spokes on a wheel, they aren't required to be in any particular order, but each plays a part in holding the wheel together. Each provides structural support that allows you to make progress in cultivating the manna mindset. If some things discussed in the fundamentals feel repetitive it's because they are. Repetition of these practices reinforce our growth.

The first fundamental is to surrender.

The second fundamental is to clear your mind to allow a new vision to emerge.

The third fundamental is to be intentional with your words, thoughts, and focus.

The fourth fundamental is to elevate your mood and physical sense of well-being—your *vibrational frequency.*

The fifth fundamental is to expect miracles. You create a sense of positive expectancy by training your thoughts to expect the best.

The sixth fundamental is to act "as if" through words and deeds.

The seventh fundamental is to stay present and follow the flow.

The eighth fundamental is to open your heart and keep it open.

The ninth fundamental is to rest and play.

SIX

∞

SURRENDER

Surrendering is allowing the Universe to express itself through you and as you.

The first fundamental to creating the manna mindset is to surrender. Stop energizing old pattern and habits that keep you stuck. Surrender to a power greater than yourself. Similar to the first step in the twelve steps of Alcoholics Anonymous, when we surrender to a source greater than ourselves, we can shift our experience. We can let go and let God.

Some people say sovereignty and surrender are incompatible. Not me. I believe it's *through* surrendering to the Divine that we gain the ability to become sovereign. When you try to do things from will or the human realm, you are limited; but when you surrender to the Divine and whatever is naturally coming forth around you, you can surf the waves of emergence and flow.

In self-defense, for example, if you can't get the upper hand when you're being attacked, you surrender temporarily. You wait and then you surge up. This surrender is known as *going to zero*. Think of surrender in these terms, as a decision, to let go momentarily and align with the Divine before you take the next step.

What the Ego Wants Versus What the Soul Needs

Manna consciousness is not a wish list. Manna consciousness is an anchoring into a consciousness of divinity that knows our soul's deepest desires for our growth and unfoldment and that's what the Universe conspires to gift us.

Our needs are always met. Not our desires.

What does it mean to get what you need?

You may have wanted to attend an Ivy League college, but you didn't get in and so you had to go to a state school. You may feel angry and betrayed by the Universe for not manifesting your dream to attend an Ivy League university. However, if you're willing to widen your view perhaps you met your best friend or your spouse at that state college. Or maybe you met a mentor who opened the next door for you. You begin to see that attending state college allowed you to connect with people who you were unlikely to have crossed paths with if you hadn't.

We can spend time focused on what didn't happen, or we can focus on what has happened and how that's ultimately been the right path for us. When we do this, we are surrendering to our soul's unfoldment, rather than indulging our egos.

There are many definitions of *the ego*. I am not using the Freudian one. The definition I'm using here is the aspect of the self that is human, mortal, and yearns to be right. It is a fragile and finite aspect of humanity concerned with image and status. It is the more narcissistic aspect of the self. The ego wants to be perceived in a particular way. The ego wants to keep up with the Joneses. It's the part of us that always finds the grass is greener.

The definition of *the soul* that I am using is the aspect of us that is immortal. Its function is to grow spiritually, to evolve in this lifetime and beyond. The soul is infinite and unfolding. People like Saint Francis, Nelson Mandela, Jimmy Carter, Mother Teresa, and Gandhi, who are known for concerning themselves with love and compassion despite their human imperfections, embody aspects of the soul's unfoldment.

Perhaps you struggle with believing in the concept of an immortal soul. Consider for a moment the possible advantages of acting as if you did believe you had one. Perhaps it would help you to be less selfish? Perhaps you would feel a connection to something deeper? Imagine what that leap of faith would give you.

I believe we are here to meet the soul's needs for growth and unfoldment, not the whims and desires of the ego. This, in and of itself, creates internal strife. These two aspects of us are often at odds with one another. One aspect wants material possessions, status, sexual conquest, adoration, and power. The other aspect strives to learn, remain unattached, fluid, and to know itself deeply and feel unified to something greater than itself. Both aspects are needed because we must survive in the material world in order to exist and have the opportunity to learn and grow. However, we must not indulge the ego and forfeit the soul's lessons. This is the work because the ego sees itself as separate.

The ego focuses on itself as an island and the soul knows that it is a wave connected with other waves in creating a vast ocean. For example, when we feel we are alone in our existential suffering, we experience our suffering alone. When we realize we are not the only one suffering, we reach out to others who are in pain.

The ego acts in isolation. The soul acts in concert. The soul understands the interconnectedness of all of life and regards all life as life unfolds around it.

As we consider our desire for anything, we need to ask ourselves, "Is this desire coming from a wish to fulfill my egoic needs? Am I craving a specific outcome or am I allowing the Universe to cocreate with me?" This is especially important to do when one is craving material objects and cash. Financial abundance is attractive to our egos because it is so highly valued in our society.

The ego may hijack our experiences with its cravings for "abundance" (a distorted concept that customarily excludes genuinely valuable things like love and human connection). We may focus on recognition and material results. We may want specific houses, lovers, awards, success in specific fields and in specific ways. We want a specific amount of money. We want what we want but we don't need those things.

It's not that receiving those things in and of themselves is a bad thing, it's just that we can see these goals are motivated from ego.

Receiving on a soul level is fundamentally different. On the soul level, we know we get what we need. We know our needs are met, even if that looks like receiving second-hand furniture. Even if that means living with a roommate.

The Universe gifts us the experiences that we need to grow. Maybe we don't get a promotion we wanted for a while because the Universe is giving us a different opportunity. Maybe we've been making our living creating things that are harmful to the planet and our soul is insisting that we can no longer remain in this field. Or we've just been kicked out of the old job to take on a new assignment, one that later elevates rather than destroys.

We may wonder what's going on, but the Universe is addressing what we need on the soul level to grow.

What Does Your Soul Need?

If you were to create some mental space, you might gain clarity on what your soul really needs. You may be surprised to find that your soul needs very little in terms of material wealth and status. It is not usually the soul that craves security. It is more likely that your soul yearns for simple happiness, connection, and purpose. Your soul yearns to grow and discover. Your soul yearns for deeper meaning and authentic expression and connection with life and the people around you. Your soul yearns to breathe and stretch.

It is your ego that wants stuff. It is your ego that craves power. It is your ego that wants things to look and be a certain way. Your soul is more surrendered. More open to the flow of life and being present from moment to moment.

The manna paradigm shift is about living from the soul. It is about our receptivity to life as it wishes to evolve around us and emerge through us. Receptivity, not struggle.

When we surrender our egoic desires, we create more space for the Universe to meet the clearly understood needs of our souls.

Surrendering isn't about giving up on our dreams or about blaming the Universe when it doesn't give us what we want. If we do that, we are engaging in victim consciousness and holding onto the belief that our lives are the way they are because bad things happen to us and we have no control over what happens to us. This belief is the lowest state of consciousness and is known in psychology as having an *external locus of control.*

The person with an external locus of control denies that their thoughts, beliefs, attitudes, and actions shape their circumstances, and they feel that they have no say in how situations unfold.

Surrendering is different. Surrendering is an emotional position you can take of allowing the Universe to express itself "through you" and "as you." Rather than blaming the Universe when things happen, it is recognizing you play a part in what happens to you.

Focus on addressing your thoughts, beliefs, and actions. Then release control and allow life to create through you. See how it feels to stop resisting being one with the energy of life itself.

Manna consciousness invites us to surrender, which involves this kind of letting go of control and insistence on specific outcomes.

Manna consciousness is not "manifestor consciousness," often equated with the film *The Secret* that popularized the hermetic principle of the *law of attraction,* which is one of many metaphysical laws in that philosophical tradition from antiquity. It's not about thinking and growing rich. It's not about making something happen.

Sometimes things don't seem to work out. If you keep trying to "make something happen," but nothing sticks, you will feel like you're banging your head into the wall—*because you are.* When your wheels are spinning in the mud and you're not getting anywhere, manna consciousness invites you to let go. Stop pressing on the gas pedal.

Letting go is not failure. Letting go means you are inviting the Universe to guide you.

Letting Go Isn't Giving Up

After you stop struggling to get something accomplished, people may say things to you that will make you feel like you're giving up. For example, they might say: "You're stupid," like my supervisor did. And this kind of judgment can feel terrible. But don't let other people be the narrators of your story. Define your own experience. They don't know what's happening inside your head and body. So, don't grant them the authority over your life.

Letting go is not "giving up," as in being a loser or a quitter. It's about being relaxed and accepting while pursuing your goals. If you have ever had a massage, there may be a moment when the massage therapist tells you to let go. The therapist might be referring to the fact that you are holding tension in your arm. That lack of relaxation is a sign that you're still trying to be in control during your massage. They mention it because it's impacting their ability to help you.

To make the manna paradigm shift you need to give up controlling anything other than your intentions, focus, and actions. You be in charge of yourself and let the Universe be in charge of itself. This allows the Universe to support you. It allows you to be guided.

Most of us have some resistance to relinquishing control. We like the idea of being in control. We have a hard time trusting, so we try to manage everything ourselves. If you think I'm wrong, try doing a trust fall where you close your eyes and fall backwards into the arms of a group of people who have promised to catch you. You might find yourself extremely resistant to letting go and falling despite their collective promise. Yet, doing this exercise builds a muscle of trust if you have trustworthy people engaged in this exercise with you.

Just as letting go is not giving up. Surrender is not "giving up" either. Surrender is giving up *control*. Surrender is giving up efforting. *Efforting* is when we try to force things to happen a certain way. Like Cinderella's stepsisters trying to force their feet into the glass slipper, efforting is trying too hard to make things work out.

Surrendering control doesn't mean you do nothing. It means you do what you need to do and then you back off. When we're in the energy of effort, we are not in the energy of alignment.

Efforting is also about trying to figure things out, which requires a heavy investment of mental energy to find solutions.

Sometimes you're "doing everything right" but you still don't have control over your success. At times like these, it's good to remember that you do have control over your mindset. Instead of efforting, conserve your energy. Take your right actions. Then back off and do what you can to relax and wait for the next right moment to act again. This is allowing.

Plant the seeds, water them, but don't dig them up. Just surrender them to the soil. It's not about inaction. It's about understanding how life takes care of itself and not forcing an outcome too soon. That way you can be prepared for what does happen, not just what you *want* to happen *when* you demand it.

Manna consciousness is a state of letting go and being mentally and emotionally receptive, open and available to the Universe to bring forth the answers in good timing. Focus on what you can do and then relax.

Follow the wisdom of the Serenity Prayer:

*"God, grant me the serenity to accept the things I
cannot change. The courage to change the things I can.
The wisdom to know the difference."*[1]

We surrender and wait. This doesn't mean we do nothing. It means we stay awake and aware. And we can surrender and act. We can keep doing our work. We can keep listening for direction. We can see how things unfold and we observe. We can wait for more information. We can wait to be clear.

Imagine someone has thrown a rock into a pristine creek and stirred up sediment that now obscures the bottom. The water is so murky that you can't see through it. That's what efforting does. It stirs up our emotional sediment. Intense emotions create murkiness in our thought processes.

We don't make decisions well when we can't see clearly. We must wait for the sediment to settle. Once we can see clearly again, whatever action we need to take will become clear.

Being surrendered helps us keep our mental waters clear. In this way, we rarely need to *make decisions* because the course of our actions usually is obvious.

Let's say your spouse has had an affair. Do you stay or go? It depends. How do you feel? Are you ready to end the marriage? Do you have strong negative feelings about the affair and your marriage and spouse? If you have strong negative feelings about the situation, your spouse, and your marriage and you're ready to end it, then that sounds like a clear "go" in your case.

However, if you're not sure you want to end your marriage or if you have mixed feelings about your spouse and the affair, then you don't have a clear-cut answer. In that case, you would want to pause and let go of trying to figure things out right then.

You don't try to fix the marriage and you don't quit the marriage. Not yet.

Instead, you allow yourself to feel your feelings. You allow the knowledge to settle in. You collect information. You register your spouse's emotional responses, such as their level of remorse, their interest in maintaining contact with the person they had the affair with, and their emotional intimacy with you.

You also take your own "temperature." How do you feel about your spouse? Do you feel angry at your spouse? Betrayed? Do you feel love and compassion for your spouse? Do you feel relieved the truth is out, relieved that you have a way out if you need it? Do you imagine yourself happier being divorced from this person?

Take it all in. Let the dust settle. Surrender the future. The days ahead will bring you more information. When the dust settles you'll be able to feel what the best course of action is.

Whatever you decide, make it an active choice.

If you choose to stay, choose it. Don't just passively remain in the marriage. If you decide to leave your marriage, that's fine too. Don't think of it as quitting or giving up. Think of it as making a new choice. A new covenant. As making a new agreement. If you've made vows like "Till death do us part," you may come to realize that there was an ending. The end of that covenant. The end of that agreement.

Now let's imagine it's a negative experience at work or multiple negative experiences at work that's at issue. How do you know if this one is the one that breaks the camel's back?

This is how I knew. When I had my negative experience at work, I expressed my outrage and voiced my concern. Then I let it go. I wasn't in the position to quit my job. I wasn't prepared mentally, emotionally, or financially. I kept living my life. I couldn't change it, so I had to surrender.

I surrendered and waited for guidance. Two years later, I got it. It became clear that I had to leave my job. The Universe did its part to send me messages:

- I was passed over for a promotion for a job I actually created (and was already doing the duties of) because I didn't include a copy of my doctoral degree with the application—although I'd had been working for the government with my Ph.D. for 13 years.

- Then if that wasn't enough, ground squirrels ravaged the wiring in my car's engine in my work parking lot on three separate occasions, costing me a total of $1,500 in insurance copayments to replace the wiring. That was when it was clear to me that the Universe didn't want me parking my car in the parking lot anymore. It was a giant hint to move on.

There were other signs, but those two were the ones that cemented my decision to leave. I had surrendered my job to the Universe and two years later received a clear answer to leave and start my own private practice. My last day at the prison was in December 2008.

By February, I had six private practice clients. I was slowly building my practice. So slowly, in fact, that my wife at the time was hoping I would go back to work at the prison. I did my part to let people know that I had a private coaching and therapy practice. However, I continued to surrender my livelihood to the Universe.

Solidly employed since I was sixteen, I had never gone for more than two weeks without a job, or several, but now I was living from manna consciousness. Instead of worrying about only having six clients, which would only contract my energy and make me appear more desperate, I decided to go on vacation. I booked an inexpensive trip to Italy. Why stay home, bored out of my mind, waiting and hoping for clients to show up, when I could enjoy the freedom I'd created for myself? This wasn't an extravagant trip, but it was a meaningful one. I saw beautiful, historic places that I'd learned about in world history courses. The trip allowed me to be present, engaged and happy. I discovered how I felt when I was living my best life.

After I returned from Rome, when I spoke with people about my trip and my surrendered approach to life, they were more attracted to working with me. They liked my relaxed confidence. My practice started to grow. I never considered working at the prison again.

I'm not suggesting that everyone should travel as part of their surrender. You have to listen to what your manna consciousness is inviting you to do or not do. This was an important part of my manna paradigm shift. I learned that whenever things feel tight or fear emerges, it's best to relax and surrender. This lesson changed my life.

Just Float

Another way of creatively building your surrender muscle would be to float in an isolation tank. An isolation tank is filled with copious amounts of salt water allowing you to float effortlessly. You can also choose to turn off the lights and float in complete darkness creating a womb-like scenario. I can't think of anything more *surrendered* on the physical level. You just let go completely.

Watsu is another practice that can help you relax and surrender. Watsu is a form of facilitated bodywork that takes place in warm water. It consists of one or more individual sessions in which a practitioner floats you on your back and gently cradles you in chest-deep warm water. It is deeply relaxing, and helps you build trust as your body is being supported by a practitioner who moves, stretches, and massages you.

Your Surrender: Self-Reflection

What's happening in your life that isn't going the way you want it to?

Where are you efforting to make things happen?

Are you going in circles?

Are you just digging yourself in deeper?

Can you soften?

Could you take your hands off the wheel and let the "car" steer itself?

Are you willing to let go?

☯

SEVEN

CLEAR YOUR MIND

Speak lovingly. Focus on the beauty. Return to the
wholeness in the here and now, and let your mind
be renewed daily.

The manna mindset comes when we can clear our minds and create space from the noise and negativity in our heads. A clear mind allows us to open and listen to our intuition, which allows us to be receptive to manna.

Just like a computer gets backed up with previous searches that slow it down, so do our minds. Our minds get junked up with old thoughts, resentments, worries, and memories. If we want to stay present, open, and available to follow the flow and receive our new supply of manna, we need to begin each day fresh. We need to clear the cache. We need to release yesterday's events from our minds.

Your goal is to release resistance and agitation, so you can anchor into renewed clarity and peace.

Meditation

Meditation is one practice that will allow you to clear your mental cache. Meditation helps you let go of whatever you're doing and whatever has occurred before you begin meditating. It will help you gather up the pieces of yourself that you've left in the past. Meditation will also bring you back if you've mentally launched yourself into the future and return you to your wholeness in the here and now.

Meditation is a powerful practice that helps us remain present in the present, which is where our power lies.

Meditation is simple. The practice involves making a conscious choice to stop all outward physical activity and to close your eyes. With your eyes closed, begin taking deep breaths and enter a state of stillness and quiet. Let your thoughts come and go with every inhalation and exhalation. Don't try to hold on to any thought or to force yourself *not* to have a thought. Simply observe their coming and going as you turn your focus inward to your breath. You can sit in the stillness for five to ten minutes (or longer), allowing your mind to begin to quiet.

A regular meditation practice will help you reset again and again.

Meditation is a spiritual practice that makes you receptive to the voice of the Higher Mind. As you quiet your own mind, you create space for the Infinite to communicate with you. This is like fine-tuning a station, so that you can receive divine inspiration and wisdom.

During meditation, you can hear more clearly. Your intuition is sharper. If prayer is speaking to God, meditation is listening. The practice of meditation not only helps clear your mind of negativity and limited thinking; it also allows you to connect with a higher frequency of consciousness. This is possible because it raises your personal vibration.

The manna mindset is enhanced by developing an ability to stop yourself from swirling around in mental states of confusion, anxiety, and self-doubt. Meditation can help. It is a mental weedwhacker. It clears space.

The more frequently and longer you meditate, the more significant its effect on your mind will be. Imagine your brain as a glass of water. Each thought you have is like air blown through a straw into this glass of water, creating bubbles. The more thoughts, the more bubbles. Once you start meditating, the flow of air through the straw lessens and your thought bubbles gradually die down. No more bubbles, only still water—and the clarity that comes with it.

There are many forms of meditation. Mindfulness, Zen, vipassana. I'm not endorsing any particular kind. Each is valuable. Explore different kinds of meditation practices and see which ones resonate with you. Then do them regularly.

Personally, I find mindfulness meditation wonderful for daily awareness and staying conscious in my life. I also appreciate the practice of vipassana meditation. *Vipassana* is a Sanskrit word that means to "see things as they are." According to the spiritual teacher Goenka, who made it known around the world, vipassana was taught in India 2,500 years ago. It includes silent, mindful breathing and self-observation.[1]

As of this writing, I have completed a silent ten-day meditation retreat and several three-day silent retreats. Ten days in silent meditation can feel challenging at times; however, at the end of the experience you are richly rewarded with a renewed mind and a deep sense of calm.

Beginning to Meditate

Here are the basics of meditation. Find a comfortable place to sit where you won't be disturbed. You may sit upright in a chair or cross-legged on the floor or a couch, whichever suits you.

Set a timer for 5–15 minutes on your phone or clock. Later, you can increase this by ten-minute increments and go up to 60 minutes if you so desire.

Close your eyes and begin taking slow easy breaths. Refrain from scratching or fidgeting if you are able. Don't be alarmed if you have a lot of thoughts—that's normal. Don't judge them. In fact, don't pay them any attention. Simply allow them to arise without fighting them. You'll find that just by observing yourself, your usual mental chatter will gradually dissipate of its own accord.

Just continue to sit still, gently breathing and relaxing your mind and body, without falling asleep.

You may find your body tingling. You may feel like your floating outside your body. Don't worry about these sensations. Just continue to breathe and let go.

You will eventually come to realize that your consciousness is not limited to your body and realize that you are more than your body. However, for now, your purpose is simply to let go and reset.

When the alarm goes off, gradually get up from your meditation spot. You should feel renewed. If you do not or if you'd like to continue, you can set the alarm for another ten-minute segment and continue.

A regular meditation practice can shift the quality of your life. Among other things, just like exercise has enormous health benefits, so does a regular meditation practice. Research has found that meditation increases mental and physical health and wellbeing.[2] It reduces stress, anxiety, negative thoughts, and depression.[3] It reduces insomnia and lowers blood pressure. There are even indications that meditation can lessen your cravings for nicotine and other addictive substances.

If you want to create a regular meditation practice, *schedule it*. You can start by creating a practice that includes meditating once per day or several times a day for short segments. For example, you might choose to meditate every morning when you wake up and every evening before dinner or bed for fifteen minutes at a pop. Or you could set aside 30–60 minutes every day for one longer meditation session.

As with all practices, consistency is important. If you are able to set up a regular time in your schedule, you will be more likely to keep this appointment with yourself and it will train your brain to recognize that it's meditation time and cooperate with you.

The most important thing is that you find a way to make meditation a regular part of your life so that you can reap its spiritual, mental, and physical health benefits.

There are also a multitude of apps and YouTube videos that can help you with meditation. Please see the Resources for some suggestions.

Earthing and Nature Therapy

In the past, people could easily hit the reset button with a walk on the beach or in the forest, locations where they were refreshed by the negative ions that filled the air. Negative ions are found in nature. They are restorative. They increase the level of serotonin in our bodies and relax us.[4] We are exposed to the negative ions at the ocean or in the mountains, near waterfalls.

Because of how we live today, in manmade environments with a lot pollution, we can no longer take for granted the ways that nature supported us in staying connected to our authentic essence and wholeness. We must be mindful of taking action to maintain our connection to the natural world.

Earthing is another practice that will help you clear your mind and come back to pure presence. Earthing is the practice of sitting, lying, or walking barefoot on grass or soil.[5] Pavement doesn't have the same electro-magnetic effects. Find some time to go lay in the grass in your yard or at a neighborhood park. If you don't have the ability to do that, find a patch of grass and take off your shoes and walk barefoot on it. Let the earth renew your energy. Earthing is a great way to hit your personal refresh button.

The practice of earthing or *grounding* is a relatively new concept. In the 20th century, people were more likely to spend time in nature, picnicking, lying on the grass, or sitting on the ground in some capacity, so they didn't need to be told to make an explicit choice to do this.

People in urban areas and those who live in apartments and drive to work in high-rises don't have much opportunity to connect with earth. This is also why concepts and terms like ecotherapy, nature therapy, forest therapy, and forest-bathing have emerged.

In the 1980s, forest-bathing was birthed in Japan, where it is called *shinrin-yoku,* a term that means "taking in the forest atmosphere."[6] According to a WebMD article, forest bathing improves mood and immunity and lowers depression levels and cortisol levels in the body.[7] It is a fantastic way to clear our minds and refresh our bodies. This refreshment lightens us. Feeling lighter contributes to our ability to engage in the other fundamentals that create the manna mindset.

Journaling

Journaling can be another way to clear the cache.

Take out a journal or notebook and just do a mind dump. Write everything out on paper. Everything you're feeling. Everything you need to let go of.

You might consider doing this with a notebook you can tear the paper out of. You can set a timer for five minutes and then just write every word or thought that enters your mind, without edits or corrections. As you write it down, imagine that you're turning it over to the Universe. When the timer goes off, tear out the pages you've written, rip them up, and throw them in the trash. Just let them go.

Some people might suggest writing everything down in a journal first thing in the morning to just let it go. However, if you find yourself starting the day with yesterday's old news and dragging the past into the present, try doing this practice at a different time of the day.

Additionally, doing a mind dump on to the page can be useful towards the end of the day—preferably a few hours before bed. You don't want to go to sleep with your head filled with your troubles that actually might cause insomnia or bad dreams. It's better to go to bed reflecting on what went well, what you're grateful for, and what you can look forward to tomorrow.

Chakra Clearing and Vocal Toning

Another practice that helps me clear negative energy and center myself is vocal toning. Vocal toning is a type of sound healing or music therapy. According to an article in the *Journal of Music Therapy*, "Toning is a form of vocalizing that utilizes the natural voice to express sounds ranging from cries, grunts, and groans to open vowel sounds and humming on the full exhalation of the breath."[8] The authors of the study found that participants' three most common descriptors of toning were "meditative," "calm," and "relaxed." My experience with toning is that it shifts the vibration in my body and helps me feel energetically in alignment and at peace, like when chanting the sound *Om*.

One toning exercise I find particularly effective is chakra chanting. I learned about this practice from the sound healer Jonathan Goldman (see Resources). Chakras are spiritual energy centers in and around the body that were first recorded in ancient Indian texts known as the Vedas which date to an era prior to 500 BCE. There are seven main chakras in the human body. Each has a corresponding color and sound.

The first or root chakra, located at the base of the spine, is red. The second or sacral chakra, located in the lower abdomen, is orange. The third chakra, located in the solar plexus, is yellow. Together these are considered the *lower chakras*.

The fourth or heart chakra, located in the chest, is green. It is considered the spiritual center of the body, acting as the fulcrum that connects the lower, earth-based chakras with the higher, celestial chakras.

The fifth chakra, located at the throat, is turquoise. The sixth chakra, also known as the third eye, located between the eyes where the eyebrows come together, is purple or indigo. The seventh or crown chakra, located just above the top of the head, is violet. These three are known as the *higher chakras.*

Toning the sound of your chakras while visualizing their colors will help you to clear these energy centers and gain access to their full power, which involves activating and raising your kundalini energy, a sacred energy that moves up the spine.

Goldman's chakra chants are seven different vocalizations for each of the seven chakras.

For the first chakra, the tone vocalized is UUH, like the vowel sound in the word "duck."

For the second chakra, the tone vocalized is OOO, like the vowel sound in the word "you."

For the third chakra, the tone vocalized is OH, like the vowel sound in the word "no."

For the fourth chakra, the tone vocalized is AH, like in the word "jaw."

For the fifth chakra, the tone vocalized is EYE, like the vowel sounds in the word "I."

The vocalization for the sixth chakra is AYE, like the vowel sound in "hay."

The tone for the seventh chakra is EEE, like the vowel sound in the word "me."9

Some mystical traditions see a connection between the chakras and the sefirot (the Tree of Life) from the kabbalistic teachings. When you clear out the static in your energy fields, you are more available to the Divine Mind. Your antenna is clear.

Other Practices for Helping You Clear Your Mind

Other practices for clearing your mind include going for a walk, swim, run, or working out at the gym. For some of us, cooking a meal or brewing a cup of tea might be the perfect way to clear out our minds. Many people find that taking a hot bath is a great way to let go. For others, doing yoga or getting a massage is a meaningful way to refresh.

What Helps You Clear Your Mind? Self-Reflection

I invite you to explore and find what works well for you as you reflect on the questions below.

What helps me let go of my worries?
What helps me feel refreshed?
What helps me begin again or reset my mind?
How has meditation helped me improve my mood?
How has physical activity helped me improve my mood?
What relaxation practices help me calm my mind?

What resources or activities would help me clear my cache and begin again with a renewed mind?

EIGHT

ꕥ

BE INTENTIONAL WITH YOUR WORDS, THOUGHTS, AND FOCUS

*Our thoughts influence every aspect of our lives from
what we talk about to what we do. Choose them wisely.*

One of the fundamental ways to begin to enter into the manna mindset and create a new joyful vision for your life is to be intentional with your thoughts, words, and focus. Prepare your mind to receive manna by addressing how you speak to yourself and others, shifting your thought patterns, and observing what you focus on as you go through your day.

Watch Your Mouth, Kid

Negative talk, whether about ourselves or others, is a destructive habit that keeps us anchored in a negative mindset and prevents us from experiencing joy or expecting good things. To be in the manna mindset requires you to stop speaking negatively about yourself, your circumstances, and other people. Not only do you want to catch yourself when you find yourself complaining, you want to stop complaining. Don't indulge in gossip, criticizing, or complaining. Can it. What's the old proverb? If you can't say anything nice, don't say anything at all.

I know this is a hard one. Several spiritual practitioners I know do an annual 21-day "no-complaints fast." The goal is to refrain from complaining for 21 consecutive days. If you complain even once, the fast starts over.

Full disclosure, I've never managed 21 consecutive days without a complaint. But I would bet if I did, I'd have an even more amazing life.

One way to create more consciousness around refraining from complaining is to set up something similar to a swear jar. You put a dollar in the jar every time you engage in complaining.

Now to be clear, appropriate feedback is not the same as complaining. There is a difference between making requests or providing feedback and criticizing someone or complaining.

Creating a powerful manna mindset also involves addressing our negative self-talk. Many of us would never think to say the things to others that we say to ourselves. Our inner critics can really rip us up. Please, dear one, put it on the top of your to-do list to stop saying negative things about yourself. This kind of self-talk is very destructive to our self-esteem and severely limits our ability to connect with manna consciousness.

When you catch yourself saying something negative about yourself, stop. Try to find a way to positively reframe the negative comment. If you just said, "I'm so stupid." Stop yourself and reword the thought positively, as, "I'm learning, and I respect myself for trying."

Or if you catch yourself saying, "No one likes me," stop yourself and reword the thought positively, as "I'm learning to like myself and there are people who like and care for me."

Don't let negative self-commentary go unchecked. It's like insulting someone and never apologizing. Correct it so you can move forward. Choose to be kind to yourself.

Positive Self-Talk and Affirmations

Positive self-talk can be a gentle way of encouraging yourself throughout the day. Self-affirmation is a kind of cheering yourself on or giving voice to an internal cheerleader who encourages you. "You're doing great, kid. I believe in you. I'm so proud of you."

Affirmations are intentional statements that you make which are intended to be positive and encouraging. You can write out your affirmations. You can keep them in your phone and post them in your car, near a mirror, or around your house. I literally have over 100 positive affirmations in my journal. I try to read them all at least twice a week out loud.

Every time I begin a new journal, I copy them by hand in the first five pages of the journal, sometimes creating new ones as I go.

Some people like to record their affirmations and then listen to them.

Whatever works for you is best.

Examples of positive affirmations are:

- "I do my best. I am smart and capable. I am a caring person making a positive difference in the lives of others."
- "I am a loving partner and parent."
- "I am healthy and happy."
- "I am surrounded by beauty and I am thriving."

What Were You Thinking?

Notice your thoughts. Our thoughts influence every aspect of our lives. In fact, if you notice what kind of mood you're in and then you notice the thoughts you've been thinking you will see a correlation. Are your thoughts uplifting you or bringing your down?

When you catch yourself thinking a negative thought, stop and redirect the negative self-talk. If you had the thought. *I totally messed up.* Stop the thought and replace it with, *No one is perfect. I did my best and I will keep trying to improve.*

If you have a diagnosed mood disorder, you may need to get more help than this book can provide you to deal with your negative thoughts and thinking errors, as well as your mood swings. If you have a mood disorder, your negative mood may be contributing to your negative thoughts and your negative thoughts may be contributing to your negative moods. You'll likely need some intervention to help you stop the circular pattern.

That said, the material presented here can help you begin to engage in helpful practices to shift both your thinking and your mood.

What Are You Looking At?

Notice what you're focusing on. Are you focusing on the pleasant aspects of life or the unpleasant ones? As you go through your day are you noticing the beauty around you or the filth? Are you aware of what works or does your mind keep drawing you to what's broken?

Look around you now and choose to focus on the beauty. Find the goodness of this moment. Enjoy where you are. Take in the grace, the warmth, the perfection of this moment. Nice, right? It feels good to notice the good.

What Do You Have to Be Grateful For?

Tune to what you are grateful for and turn up your level of appreciation for the good things in your life. The more you're tuned to the channel of appreciation, the better you'll feel. Programming your mind to be appreciative and to focus on gratitude and what there is to be grateful for in every moment will shift your reality.

These are the types of practices that create the manna mindset.

Allow a New Vision to Emerge: A Guided Meditation

As you read and follow the advice given here in *The Manna Paradigm Shift*, a new vision of what's possible for your life will emerge. It is my hope that you'll decide that you will no longer subscribe to the old reality. That you'll begin to envision *a new reality* in which people are valued, housed, and have medical care. One in which everybody values people over profits. One that includes time to connect with one another and our families. A new reality where we are not cogs in a machine.

We must do this on the macro level and on the micro level.

Now I invite you to begin this meditation. Take some deep breaths, get calm and peaceful. Tap into love. Then read each sentence and visualize what it says as you go along. Later you can write down each sentence as an affirmation. If you would like to hear a prerecorded audio of this meditation, please visit my YouTube channel (see Resources).

Begin to reimagine your life. Imagine living your life with all of your needs met.

You live in a safe and comfortable home.

You have time to connect with your friends, partner, children, family.

You have time for creative pursuits.

Your body is healthy, and you have time to exercise, meditate, walk, and connect with nature.

You have time and the resources to invest in nurturing self-care practices, massage, acupuncture, yoga.

You have excellent health care.

Your food is healthy and organic.

You have time to prepare and cook your meals with healthy ingredients.

You easily pay your bills.

You feel respected on the job and are meaningfully sharing your gifts and talents.

You are sufficiently compensated for your contributions and treated with respect and acknowledgement.

Your work is an important aspect of your life, but not the only or most important aspect.

You feel good about the ways you show up, contribute to others and keep peace and balance in the world.

You feel happy and fulfilled.

A New Vision for Your Life: Self-Reflection

Take a moment to reflect on the following questions and then write out your answers in your journal.

What do you love about your life?

What would you like more of?

What would you like to release or what would you like less of?

What do you want to spend your day doing?

Who do you want to spend your time with?

What kind of work do you want to do?

How many hours a week do you really want to work?

Where would you like to live?

What changes would you like to see in your surroundings?

What changes do you want to see in your community, your town, your country, the world?

What changes are you willing to make to better your surroundings and create the kind of community you'd like to create?

NINE

ᕦᕤ

ELEVATE YOUR MOOD AND RAISE YOUR VIBRATIONAL FREQUENCY

Feeling abundant, free, and joyful connects you to manna consciousness.

As we discussed in the last chapter, creating a manna mindset requires you to be intentional with your thoughts and focus. This is not denying the things in your life that aren't as you'd like them. It means focusing on the things in your life that are good. By being intentional, you can create an elevated feeling state or vibrational frequency in your body.

What Is Vibrational Frequency?

Vibrational frequency is a combination of your mood and your energy level. Your vibration can be positive or negative. When you are feeling energized and in a positive mood or elevated state of emotion as defined below your vibration or frequency is fast and high. When you are feeling lethargic and your mood is sullen, angry, sad, or dissatisfied, your vibration is slow and your frequency is low.

When others come into your energy field they will be aware, consciously or unconsciously, of how you feel. Your energy or vibration can influence other people's moods. It can uplift others, or it can put others in a bad mood.

As I was editing this book for its final review I heard spiritual teacher Michael Bernard Beckwith state in a service before the November 2020 U.S. election that in today's world "your frequency is your currency. Your frequency is your destiny." I couldn't agree more. This is true whether we are pre-, post-, or mid-pandemic, recession, or depression. Our energetic frequency influences our life experiences. Anchoring into manna consciousness requires a higher vibration or frequency.

You can create a high, fast, and clear energy frequency in your body by engaging in practices that create an elevated feeling state.

What Is an Elevated Feeling State?

Elevated feelings include joy, love, peace, appreciation, enthusiasm, exuberance, excitement, bliss, and happiness. When you are feeling these elevated emotions, you are in a state where the potentiality to attain manna consciousness is heightened.

It is not possible to achieve manna consciousness from a low vibrational frequency. Elevated feeling states, high energy frequency, or high vibration are the states that connect you to manna consciousness.

Manna consciousness is like a flow state. In manna consciousness you are connected to intuition and guidance, and as author and intuitive Penney Pierce says, your "life unfolds effortlessly and in alignment with your destiny."[1]

In the documentary *Heal*, stem cell biologist Bruce Lipton says, "The conscious mind is the creative mind. The subconscious is the default program."[2] My understanding of his statement is that our conscious mind, the one we have control over, is the mind that connects with the Divine Mind. This is the mind that creates, while the subconscious mind is the slave or servant mind, defaulting to what we are socially programmed to think.

If we want to be free we need to be intentional with our thoughts. If we want to be in the flow, we have to change where our subconscious mind is hanging out. For example, we need to consciously think thoughts that reflect the kind of reality we want to create and engage in actions in which we feel good about ourselves and our lives.

We need to stay in an elevated feeling state. As we maintain this state, we can connect with manna consciousness and bring down the good stuff from heaven. This is our path to sovereignty.

How do we stay open and available to our good, our "daily bread" as the Bible might say? We have to pivot our thinking and create higher vibrational thought and feeling patterns. We have to create thought forms that create the vibrational frequency of abundance, freedom, and joy. These are habits that lend themselves to manna consciousness.

We must engage in regular practices to raise our vibration. Just like physical exercise helps an athlete create muscle memory, doing these exercises helps the practitioner create emotional memory.

Overcoming Gravity and Shifting Your Frequency

We are all subject to gravity. Gravity is the force that keeps us tethered to the earth.

We also experience emotional gravity. Emotional gravity includes negativity bias, where we focus on and remember the bad aspects of something. Perhaps it's no mistake that the word *gravity* is a synonym of *seriousness*. The Latin root word, *gravis* means "heavy."

We tend to depress ourselves, rather than allow ourselves to feel elevated feelings. We feel the need to justify our reasons for feeling good and expect others do the same. If someone were to ask us, "Why are you so happy today?" we might be apologetic about feeling good, downplaying our happiness lest we make them uncomfortable or envious.

Manna consciousness is not found at low energetic or emotional frequencies.

You're not going to experience what manna consciousness has to offer if you're depressed or angry. You need to be able to shift your frequency—elevate your mood.

Shifting your frequency is like changing your internal channel. If you're tuned to a hard rock station, you're only going to hear hard rock music. That's fine if you want to listen to hard rock music, but you wouldn't expect to hear smooth jazz there. If you want to tune to manna consciousness, you have to change your channel to an elevated state.

Tune In

When we connect with Divine Mind or God Consciousness, we are able to connect to the unified field. It's one of those things that is hard to describe to someone who has never experienced this. Like when someone tries to tell me how to blow a bubble with gum. I've never been able to do this, and I probably never will. I can see it though, so I know it happens.

Again, when I speak of God, I'm not talking about something separate or outside of us. I'm speaking about a presence, a consciousness within us, a frequency that we connect with by energetically connecting our minds with the Divine Mind.

Perhaps you're skeptical about this because you've never felt this yet. You've only heard about it from those who've experienced it, and you can't see the tangible proof. I want to acknowledge your skepticism. I can't promise you that you're going to experience it. I can only tell you about it. I can also give you the best directions I know on how to get there and a description of what it's like to experience it. Then you can attempt to experience it for yourself.

It's like listening to the Four Stairsteps sing "Ooh Child" telling you that things are going to get easier and brighter. You can listen to that song and let it elevate you. You can let the music and lyrics create a positive feeling that life will get better and brighter. As you do, you may start to feel more comfortable in your body. You might feel more relaxed. You might feel a warmth in your heart and let the song put a smile on your face. It might start to create a feeling of certainty and positive expectancy about the future.

Or you can just hear a song, change the channel, or let the sound be background noise and remain unaffected by it.

The choice is up to you.

If you're not already at a receptive frequency, or blocking it like a know-it-all teenager, it won't resonate with you. You may be blocking it because it feels safer not to believe. You don't want to feel like a fool, so you protect yourself from believing or use reason to analyze the possibility away. However, if you're open and allowing, you will start to feel it. You can lean in. It will amplify. It will expand. And then, you're in the groove with it.

How Do You Raise Your Vibrational Frequency?

To raise your vibrational frequency, you do things that create a positive mindset and feelings in your body. You can write down what you're grateful for and what you appreciate. You can even connect with future gratitude. You can take deep, cleansing breaths. You can sing or dance. You can go for a walk or jog. You can do any physical activity that brings you joy. You can get a hug, pet your cat or dog. You can make a cup of tea or coffee or cook a beautiful meal. You can watch a comedy or read a book.

You want to feel energetically lighter in your mind and body. So, whatever works to improve your mood and mindset, you do it. Your number one goal here is to stay positive. Figure out what that is for you. It could even be helpful to know what that is for the people closest to you, so that you can remind them, and they can remind you, if either of you get in a funk.

Raise Your Vibrational Frequency

Here are some more suggestions for raising your vibrational frequency and helping you get into an elevated mood.

Meditate: Sit still and quiet your mind. Do any of the practices from the previous chapter on clearing your mind.

Listen to or play music: What music elevates your mood? What songs bring you joy? What songs help you connect with a feeling of expansion and freedom? What songs tap into your love of life? Gratitude? What songs lift you up? Create a "Joy Jams" play list.

Exercise: When we walk, jog, or run, we also return the body to its organic rhythms and come back to ourselves. Whether we are lifting weights and feeling our strength or stretching or exploring our flexibility, exercise is a powerful practice to restore our inner balance and raise our vibrational frequency. Studies have found that exercise relieves depression and, in less severe cases, is as effective as medication in treating it.[3] This is why psychologists (who are not permitted to prescribe medications like psychiatrists do) "prescribe" gym memberships, yoga, Zumba, or another form of exercise three or four times a week.

Dance: Dancing brings us joy. It feels great to connect with music while matching the rhythms with our movements. Put on some music and dance in your bedroom or kitchen. Go out with friends or by yourself to a club. Take a formal dance class or lessons or put on some line-dancing videos on YouTube and boot, scoot, and boogey. It's all about having fun and feeling good in your body.

Sing: Singing releases endorphins in our body. When we sing, we are opening up the diaphragm, which releases tension, and allows our bodies to take in more oxygen. It has benefits similar to those of deep breathing. That's why car karaoke, no matter how off-key you are singing, makes you feel good. Singing in a group is also a great way to connect with others.

Laugh: Laugher also releases endorphins. Prioritize comedy in your life. Go to comedy shows. Watch funny videos or TV. Surround yourself with people who are funny and good-natured.

Speak Affirmations: Affirmations are positive statements that help us program our thoughts. For example, you could say, "I am supported by a loving Universe that is looking out for me. I am available to more joy than I've ever felt. Things are always working out for me. I accept my good and I am magnetic to love, prosperity, and good health!" If you say it enough times with conviction, you will come to believe it and, more importantly, to live it.

Revisit "Your Mind on Manna and Manna on Your Mind" in chapter 5 (see page 44).

Connect: Call up a friend. Get out into the world. Engage with others in a real way. Much of what takes us out these days is the news and social media. Consider taking a break from socializing via social media apps and have a real connection with a real friend. Being with people you care about and who care about you will raise your vibrational frequency. Go offline and connect live.

What Helps You Raise Your Vibrational Frequency? Self-Reflection

What allows you to feel a greater level of joy?
What can you do to elevate your emotions?
Write down ten things you can do elevate your mood and feel good in your body.

EXPECT MIRACLES

*Choose to expect the best. Miracles occur when we
trust in the goodness of the Universe.*

One of the fundamental ways to create a manna mindset
and connect with manna consciousness is to program
your mind to expect miracles. Expecting miracles
requires you to create a mindset of positive expectancy.
In other words, in every situation, expect the best.

As you take steps toward your freedom, obstacles will
appear that seem insurmountable. Going back to our
allegory of the Exodus, after the Hebrew slaves escaped
their enslavement in Egypt, they came to the Red Sea.
They had no way to cross and Pharaoh's soldiers were
right behind them. Standing on the shore, Nashon, a
man whose name means "that foretells or that
conjectures" in Hebrew, stepped into the water. He
trusted that if God told Moses the people would be free
then God would make a way even where no way seemed
possible. Nashon had faith.

Nashon walked into the water and kept walking
forward. As the story is told, when the water filled
Nahshon's nostrils and he was about to drown, the

waters of the Red Sea began to part. The Hebrews made it across the Red Sea to freedom.

It was a miracle.

I want to take a moment here to bring your attention to the fact that Nashon, the one who trusted God, had formed a positive conclusion. He had faith that his circumstances would improve. He believed.

Miracles can occur in our own lives when we stay on the path of faith and trust in the goodness of the universe.

You must have faith. The English word *faith* comes from the Latin word *fides,* which means "to trust, to have confidence in." Taking steps towards your freedom is easier if you believe you live in a friendly universe that supports you. Then, like Nashon, you begin to "act as if" and take a first step, then a second step, then the next.

Watch and you'll find that the Universe makes a way for you.

As the actor Jim Carrey says, "You can spend your whole life imagining ghosts worrying about the pathway to the future, but all there will ever be is what's happening here, and the decisions we make in this moment, which are based in either love or fear."[1] Choose love and move forward with faith.

Experiencing Miracles

One of the participants in my It's Never Too Late to Be Your Self workshops shared a story about how before the Affordable Care Act of 2010, her husband lost his job and they didn't have enough money to put him on her health insurance or to pay the COBRA payments to keep him on his former employer's health insurance.

"We decided he would go without health insurance, and if he got sick, he could go on Medicare," Renee shared, referring to the federal health insurance plan. The group listened intently wondering where this story was going. "But then," Renee continued soberly, "my husband had a heart attack and he had to be airlifted via helicopter to the hospital, where they took him into surgery. Twenty-two hours later he was gone." The room gasped.

Her husband's hospital bills totaled a quarter of a million dollars. The participants shook their heads. The helicopter flight alone must have been "outrageously expensive" since they lived in a small town in Oregon and the nearest hospital was at least an hour away.

Renee said she didn't know how she was going to pay the medical bills. "They would come in the mail and I would set them aside on the table and leave them. They kept coming in and I kept stacking them up in a pile. Every time I would just give them over to the Universe. I would say, 'Universe, I don't know how to pay these bills, but I know you do.'"

We were hanging on her every word at this point, shaking our heads at how frightening that must have been for her and how helpless she must have felt.

Renee took a deep breath and continued. "Then, one day, it was time to go back to work. I needed to get back on my feet. I called my boss and said. 'I need to come in. I don't know if I can see any customers right now, but I'll do my best.'"

She described her boss as compassionate and said that her boss told her, "That's fine. Come on in and do what you can do."

Renee went to work and later that day her boss approached her and said that there were some clients there who really wanted to see her. Renee agreed to meet with the clients. She was in customer service and it was a few of the people from the hospital that her husband had died in, that had also happened to be one of the agencies she worked with. These clients brought her flowers and gave her their condolences. Then as they were leaving, one of the women turned and smiled and said, "About those bills."

Renee nodded, knowing she needed to get them paid.

"A charity took care of them," the woman said. Then she handed her an invoice with a zero balance. And just like that, a quarter of a million dollars' worth of bills were gone. She was free from that debt.

The group was speechless. This woman had experienced a miracle. She didn't inherit $250,000. She didn't win the lottery. She wasn't given a physical amount of $250,000, but all of that money came to her in a unique way—$250,000 of debt wiped away.

Renee also shared that later that same week when she was calling the credit card company to get her husband's name off their shared credit card, the customer service agent told her that there was a death benefit on the card. "What does that mean?" she asked. The agent asked the date of her husband's death and told her that all of the charges before his death would be paid by the insurance benefit. In that one phone call, $6,000 worth of credit card debt got wiped away.

While Renee still experienced the death of her husband, she shared with the group, what I've been sharing with you in this book: The Universe takes care of us. And when we are struggling, although we may not see a way, the Universe always has a way. Our needs are met one day at a time.

We can do our part to increase miracles in other people's lives through doing acts of kindness. Whose angel will you be? Whose prayers will you answer?

While I was writing this book, a friend of mine who drove Uber to supplement her income and was struggling with finances, shared with me that she had accidentally put oil in her car where the steering wheel fluid went. She was totally distraught and went immediately to a mechanic. My friend was distressed that she'd ruined her car. Not only would she be unable to earn her wages the next day, she also would be unable to pay the mechanic. The mechanic sucked out the oil, and in the process, discovered cracks in her radiator. If she had answered a ride call the next day, she would have been stranded. He made the repairs and when she asked how much it would cost, he told her zero. He was happy to help another person out. I should add that she put out a prayer request to her friends for resources to pay for the car repairs. Her prayers were answered in an unexpected way. We were all surprised and pleased for her.

Shifts and Transitions Can Create Space for Miracles

Sometimes we view a change as negative. When something ends unexpectedly, we consider it a bad thing, misfortune, or even failure. Yet, unexpected endings or changes of plan can create space for miracles. For example, when my friend Nancy lost her job doing accounting for a medical doctor after nearly a decade, she was stunned. She'd given this woman her best and the doctor wasn't an easy person to work with. But she decided to start her own payroll and accounting business and put her services out there to other doctors and mental health professionals and within a year she doubled her income. She took on more clients and was helping more people with their billing. She'd gone from barely getting by to being in the position to be able to purchase her first home. This is truly a demonstration of the old saying "When one door closes, another one opens."

Keep the Faith: Self-Reflection

Ask yourself these questions.
What thoughts would give me more courage?

What thoughts would give me more faith in myself?
What thoughts would give me more faith in life?
What thoughts would give me more space, more freedom?
What examples exist in my life or in others' lives that would give me more faith?

ELEVEN

ACT "AS IF"

*When you make an "I am" statement you begin to
create that reality.*

Another fundamental of manna consciousness is to
adopt the behaviors of someone who knows they are
provided for. Act "as if" all your needs are met. Act "as
if" what you want is going to happen. Visualize it and
then create a feeling of certainty in your body that what
you need and what you want to create in your life is
coming to pass.

The I AM Presence

When Moses was alone in the desert, God appeared
to him as a burning bush and told him to go back and
free the Hebrews, Moses asked, "Who should I say sent
me?"

God answered, "I AM that I AM."

These are power words. This phrase means that
whatever you claim for yourself you are that. If you make
an "I am" statement with your words, your thoughts, or

most powerfully, your feelings, you are connecting with your personal agency to create that reality.

For example, if you say, "I am poor," you begin to create the state of poverty in your life. By contrast, if you say, "I am prosperous," that is the reality you begin to create for yourself.

Anytime we utter the phrase *I am that* followed by a description of something, we begin to create the *that* to which we are referring.

Now let's not get overly simplistic here. I am not saying that if you say, "I am a frog," you will turn into an amphibian. I am saying that we connect with the power to create reality when our thoughts, feelings, and energy are in alignment with one another on a particular subject. This is why when we act "as if" we are paving the road to our future. We have the choice to pave our future with either desirable, positive intentions or undesirable, negative ones.

Let me explain what the effects of this power would look like in real time.

If you're hungry, feel full first. Imagine what it feels like when you have a full belly. Breathe as if you've just had a satisfying meal. After a good meal would you stretch or yawn? Would you pat your stomach? Would you recline? Would you belch? Imagine it and do it.

It's in the "feeling full" first that you create the reality of having been fed, the reality of fullness.

Letters to Juliette

Before I met my girlfriend, Diana, I was on a writing retreat in Italy. I was still nursing a bit of a broken heart, feeling sorry for myself and wondering if I would ever find true love again. Part of my mission on this trip was to visit Juliette's balcony in Verona. If you're familiar with Shakespeare's play *Romeo and Juliet,* you'll recall that she stands on her balcony and calls out for Romeo. This balcony and a statue of Juliette (Juliet) in the courtyard below have become a pilgrimage site for lovers and romantics who travel there and leave Juliette love letters. In the letters, they ask Juliette to act as a matchmaker or intercessor on their behalf and bless their love lives, so that they may find new love. I carried a few letters for friends and one that I wrote for myself to this destination.

The mythology is that if you bring a letter to Juliette and rub the left breast of her statue in the garden it will bring your true love to you.

Well, I did both. However, I took it a step further.

I spent a good part of the rest of the day touring Verona with the energetic imprint of my true love on my arm. As I walked the cobbled streets, strolled along the Adige River and ascended to the Piazzale Castel San Pietro, I imagined my beloved with me, holding my arm as I walked. I literally felt the energy of my unseen beloved. It was palpable. It felt like the energy of God, an embodied divine feminine companion, hanging on to my arm. I felt giddy. I was in the frequency of love. I could literally feel the perfect companion for me and the perfect relationship.

It was at that moment that I understood what mystical Persian poets Hafiz and Rumi must have felt when they wrote about their relationship with the Beloved (their name for God). The connection was material, tangible. I did not feel alone. I felt such a powerful presence of love with me. It was delightful. You might be thinking that I was totally delusional and that this sounds absurd at best. This is the power we have to create. I had achieved the vibrational frequency of love and I knew that I had the power to create it. The following year, I fell in love with Diana. It started when she touched my arm as we were walking.

Tap the Vibrational Frequency of Abundance and Freedom

It is my contention that everyone has an upper limit on what they will allow themselves to experience in every area of life. Like setting the thermostat in your home at a certain temperature, the place where you get stuck is your *setpoint*. Your setpoint is your current capacity for doing something. For example, how much weight you can lift, if you're weightlifting. It's getting clear on where you are now and where your abilities lie. You can also see it as where you are energetically or emotionally most of the time. Anything above your set point is out of your current comfort zone.

One of the practices I do with my clients is to help them find their current setpoint in different areas of their life, and then work with them to expand their openness and capacity for experiencing greater abundance, love, and joy. Once we establish their set point, their job is to take next steps toward their goals when they're feeling inspired and expanded rather than desperate and agitated.

In other words, their job is to move forward on days and in moments when they feel good and are embodying a higher vibrational frequency.

Let me give you an example. My client Lela had worked at as a legal secretary for many years and then left her job to work as a nanny for a family. Single and childless herself, she cherished being connected to a loving family and a child she adored. But more importantly, Lela had taken the job because it paid well, and she enjoyed the freedom her job provided. She loved taking the child on outings rather than being stuck behind a desk, taking dictation and filing papers all day. She hated deskwork and liked being out and about. Lela felt grateful that she was making more than minimum wage even without a college degree.

After a few years, Lela realized that she wanted to do something more with her life, but not for less money. I asked her to tell me how much she made and then I did a visualization process with her that focused on what it would feel like to do work that she loved. After the visualization process, I had her say "I make $___ an hour," starting with her current hourly rate and going up in increments of ten dollars.

As she made these statements, she became more comfortable with the notion of making more money. I continued this process with her until she felt she could comfortably receive twice as much as she was currently making.

I've found that while many people want to make more money, not everyone is comfortable receiving more money. Many people struggle with feeling unworthy. This was true for Lela. I helped Lela work through her resistance to receiving more money.

When Lela could feel the vibration of making twice as much as she was making at her current job, I knew she could now bring that down from heaven so to speak. She was now living in the I AM consciousness of manifesting that new level of income for herself. I invited her to start acting "as if" she was making that kind of money. I suggested she think and breathe and interact with the world "as if" she was making twice as much as she was then making.

A few weeks later, she emailed to tell me she'd received a call from a friend of hers who worked for an inspection company. They needed inspectors to go out and view properties for safety compliance. Lela applied for the job and got it. The pay was twice her current hourly pay and included benefits. She gave notice at her nanny job and took the position.

Lela contacted me six months later to tell me she loved her new job. Several months after that, she contacted me again to tell me that she had received a promotion. She expressed her gratitude to me for helping her "give herself a raise."

I had another client, May, who was struggling with raising her rates, which were not the lowest, yet neither were they on par with other successful professionals in her field. I did a visualization process with her and asked her to give herself a $50-an-hour raise. I had her imagine and feel what it was like getting paid that amount. Then I had her imagine a raise of $40, $30, $20, then $10 an hour more than she was currently charging going from highest to lowest to increase her sense of safety. It was important that she become comfortable with each amount. As I went down from $50 she noticed that she was already comfortable with lower numbers and that a $10 raise was a breeze. She could easily see herself charging and receiving $10, $20, even $30 more than she'd been charging.

I asked May to once again visualize making $50 an hour and return to the feelings of making $50 more an hour. She noticed that she soon felt comfortable with the idea of receiving $50 more an hour. As a result of the second visualization of that amount, she raised her rates. May moved from a brief moment of acting "as if" she was making $50 more in the visualization process to then charging $50 more for her services.

Beth knew she had to do something different, so she hired me as her life coach to help her get unstuck. Beth came to me depressed and defeated. She'd just completed a documentary film and was going through creative postpartum. I'm familiar with the down mood of creative postpartum. It's a real feeling that accompanies the birth of big projects like books, art installations, films, business startups, and graduate degrees because of suddenly having a loss of purpose. I've worked with many writers who have this. I also saw this phenomenon among the pre- and postdoctoral psychology interns I used to supervise, who would become depressed after graduating.

Among other things, the period right after finishing a big project, is a time when people experience great doubt and anxiety. It's a time when people may also experience the imposter syndrome and feel like a fraud. They feel depressed and lost. Unmoored.

I recognized creative postpartum immediately in Beth. The documentary had taken years to complete and now that it was done she was experiencing a sense of loss, accompanied by feelings of doubt that it would be successful. Beth was in *mitzrayim* ("narrow straits"), feeling blocked by beliefs and negative self-talk that her project wasn't good enough and that frankly neither was she. She was mentally unable either to feel a sense of accomplishment or to move forward with confidence.

When Beth came to me my first goal was to address her negative self-talk and paralyzing thoughts that she was worthless and unsuccessful and that her documentary would be worthless and fail too. I had to help her shift her vibrational frequency. Once she was in a better place emotionally, I led her through some guided meditations, and we worked on shifting her thoughts and envisioning a productive, happy future. By trusting in a happier future and beginning to imagine possibilities she previously thought were impossible, Beth was opening to the Higher Mind. She was beginning to have faith in something bigger than herself and she was pulling herself out of her self-created mental cage. My focus was to help Beth shift her repetitive thoughts that ensnared her and help her connect with her proverbial land of milk and honey. I asked her to imagine what she wanted, to picture her documentary being shown at festivals and sold in museums and specialty bookstores around the country, as well as online. I had her picture people sharing with her how much they loved her documentary. This was easy for her to envision because she'd gotten so many supporters on her crowd-funding, so she already felt what it was like to have raving fans. Beth just needed to be able to hold on to that feeling and magnify it. Her work was to get into the manna mindset and stay there.

I held the frequency of manna for her. I knew that if she were willing to believe in herself as a competent filmmaker, even a little, she could create a successful outcome for her documentary. We explored what success might look like to her and Beth identified that she wanted her film to be distributed by a specific company.

This was when I began to engage Beth in acting "as if." I had her picture her documentary being carried by that distributor and I had her imagine the amount of money she wanted to get from the distributor. "See that amount of money on a contract," I told her. We worked with her consciousness through visualization and elevating her vibrational frequency until she could see it and feel it. Beth felt empowered.

Once she felt empowered, she was ready to take steps. Beth reached out to her preferred distributor with an email about her documentary and to her amazement the company responded back that week with an offer that thrilled her.

In just a few sessions, Beth had left the narrow straits of her Egypt behind her. If she had remained in her narrow, limited thinking, that she was a failure and that her film was worthless, she would not have taken the next steps to contract the distributor.

When we stay in our enslaved thinking, we play small. We don't have faith in ourselves or our futures. We are risk adverse. We don't want to step out of line. We just keep doing what we've always done. When we free ourselves from this limited thinking and connect with the infinite possibilities of Higher Mind and manna consciousness, that power within us all, we begin to shift our realities. The substance of our lives shifts. Doors open.

Actress Racquel Bailey put faith in herself and took a risk. She invested $2,000 to purchase several billboards with her face on them in Atlanta advertising herself as a performer to get the attention of filmmaker and producer Tyler Perry whose studios are located there. It was a big, audacious idea and it paid off. Not only did she land twenty auditions after she launched her billboard campaign, she booked three roles, including one with Perry. She didn't wait for someone to give her an opportunity, she put faith in herself and created one.

This is not to suggest that all actors should buy billboards to launch their careers, as that would be absurd. What this story illustrates is the importance of listening to our own inner guidance and then acting "as if" what you want to create *is possible for you*, followed by taking aligned action. It also advises us that nothing will change if we just keep doing the same old things and thinking the same old limiting and self- deprecating thoughts. We must have a higher vision for ourselves and our possibilities if we want to free ourselves from limitations. In other words, limitations will continue to exist for us if we continue to believe we are limited.

Visualization with Emotional Association

Identify something you want to shift in your life and then try this activity. Find some time and space where you can be alone and undisturbed. Sit or lie down and close your eyes. Relax. Begin breathing deeply and easily.

As you take some relaxed breaths, think of something or someone you love and let yourself feel that love. Allow that love to relax your heart and your body even more.

As you feel your heart open begin to imagine whatever new reality you want to create.

- If you want to have harmony within your family, imagine being with your family laughing on the couch, hanging out at the beach, or enjoying each other's company at the dinner table.
- If you want to see yourself in your ideal profession visualize yourself at work doing the job in a relaxed and competent fashion (for instance, checking someone's blood pressure, performing surgery, walking clients through a home for sale, saying lines on stage, singing in a recording studio, speaking in a court room, opening your shop in the morning, standing in front of your students, programming a computer, creating a storyboard or writing a scene for your film script while sipping a cup of coffee).
- If you want to be married, imagine yourself saying your vows. See it and hear it. Feel it.
- If you want to relocate to a new city, imagine yourself walking down the streets of that city or celebrating an important holiday in that city.

Allow yourself to feel the emotions you would feel that suit the moment you're imagining. Notice what happens.

Take a moment to write down what you notice as you envision yourself in the reality you want to create.

Identify the Vibrational Frequency: A Practice

Another way to shift your energy is to take deep breaths and relax your body. Open your heart and connect with the emotion of love. Then imagine what the vibrational frequency of what you want to experience/attain might feel like.

For example, *What does the vibrational frequency of health feel like? What does the vibrational frequency of wealth feel like?*

Take some time to let yourself feel the frequency.

TWELVE

STAY PRESENT AND FOLLOW THE FLOW

To receive manna, stay present and follow the flow.
Staying present in positive expectancy is the best gift
we can give ourselves.

As you choose freedom for yourself and embark on a new path that involves making new choices for your life, you will enter a time of great uncertainty. To receive manna at that moment, you have to stay present and allow things to unfold. You have to trust the process and expect the best from the Universe.

There will always be a period of time before what you want for your life comes into your reality. It might be a second. It might be a year. It may also depend on what your wish or desire is, and factors like the laws of nature, your feelings of worthiness, etc. During this period, something intangible is happening that leads to the fulfillment of your desire. Just like when you plant a seed, and it takes time to grow. Just like when a woman is pregnant, before the baby is born, there are nine months of gestation in the womb. Gestation is a time of expectancy and preparation for what will come. Be still and know. You have to stay present and be patient. Also remember, being still is not the same as being stuck.

Get comfortable with being okay with the liminal state. *Liminal* means to be at a point of transition, in between something. According to the Oxford English Dictionary, *liminal* is from the Latin word *limen*, meaning "threshold."[1]

The word *liminality* was coined by anthropologist Arnold van Gennep to describe the phases of cultural rites of passage.[2] Choosing freedom for yourself is such a rite of passage and it will create a period of uncertainty and ambiguity in your life before the new way takes hold. Stay mentally prepared and have a mindset of positive expectancy.

Sometimes we attack ourselves when things don't instantly manifest; we blame the "delay" on our worthiness. We ask, *What's wrong with me?* and find fault that what we desire hasn't materialized. We decide we are flawed because we didn't get *that* job, *that* relationship, or *whatever* it is we wanted whether that desired thing, experience, or relationship was for our highest good or not.

This is where we learn to discern the difference between being a human being versus being a human doing. We've come here to be, not just do. We have intrinsic value. But in a capitalistic society built on slavery, humans are valued based on their acts of production, their human doing, not their human being. We have been judged by and continue to judge ourselves and other's worth based on our net worth or our ability to produce and contribute. We may all be created equal, but we are not all valued equally in a capitalistic culture.

You may recall that I mentioned that the ancient Hebrews upon breaking their chains fled into the desert. This point of transition and liminality is your proverbial desert.

The desert is a metaphor for emptiness. It appears desolate, but it is a place teeming with life. Life that burrows, blends, and conceals itself during the day and reveals itself at night.

The desert is spacious. The desert is quiet and still, a place for meditation and contemplation. The desert is where you go for vision quests to clear your mind.

The desert is a blank screen. What will you project on to it? Will you project thoughts that build confidence and courage or thoughts of failure?

The period of liminality is also a time we can call *going into the wilderness* or *wandering in the wilderness*.

Wandering in the Wilderness

When we leave a toxic relationship, a joyless job, or even stop an addiction, we will feel uncomfortable. We've left our routine behind. We feel lost. We will start to doubt our decision to leave.

This is where many of us feel like giving up.

In the story of Exodus, the Hebrews became angry with Moses for talking them into leaving Egypt. "And the whole congregation of the children of Israel murmured against Moses and Aaron in the wilderness."3 Wandering in the desert made them look back fondly on the benefits of their bondage. They enjoyed the kind of predictability that people in the military and prison experience in exchange for their freedom.

Without the comforts of the flesh that Pharaoh had provided them, they began to have more credence in Pharaoh's ability to provide for them than God's. "And the children of Israel said unto them: Would that we had died by the hand of the Lord in the land of Egypt. When we sat by the fleshpots, when we did eat the bread to the full. For ye have brought us forth into this wilderness to kill the whole assembly with hunger."4 They went into *lack consciousness,* a mindset that focuses exclusively on what's missing, what's not working out, and an inability to imagine anything improving.

We can leave those aspects of our life that limit us, and yet, continue to think in old ways that delay our joy, possibly indefinitely.

We must be patient. We cannot expect instant gratification. We also need to shield ourselves from needing to impress others and worrying about what they think. In these moments, you only want to let in the advice and opinions of people who really matter to you. Don't let peer pressure impact you. Modify your idea of success and let life unfold.

Preparations for the Journey

We can take measures to prepare us for this liminal part of the transition process. Preparations can be internal, such as creating the manna mindset, the right psychology for dealing with your time in this period.

Preparation can also be tangible, coming in the form of outside resources. However, for many people, having more financial resources doesn't make them less frightened. Some people I have worked with had more of a safety net than I had when I made my exodus from my prison job, while others had less.

No matter how many precautions you take you can't have your freedom until you take that first step. You still have to go into the proverbial desert. If you don't put yourself in a position that requires faith you'll never have a demonstration of manna.

Present-Moment Living

You could call the manna paradigm shift shifting into present-moment living, where you take everything one day at a time. What's this like? You can make plans for your future, but you remain open to change. When you do make plans, you do it from feeling into that decision. You ask: *Does this feel like the right decision now?* In other words, *right now* do you feel like it's the right decision to book a trip to Mexico in December.

If it doesn't feel right in this moment, don't assume it will be a good trip in December. Wait until you have clarity, and your decision feels right.

You want to make decisions when they feel in alignment with you.

Present-moment living is about following the breadcrumbs and listening deeply to your intuition, to your inner guidance. When you're in the desert, you have to take things one step at a time, like a rabbit. The rabbit takes a leap, stops and assesses, and then takes another leap.

In his book *Animal-Speak*, Ted Andrews talks about the spiritual wisdom of the rabbit. He says the rabbit is notable for "fertility and new life" and "moves "primarily by hops and leaps."[5] When we are in the desert, we would be well-advised to take a leap, stop and assess, and then take another as we feel guided to.

Margarita's story, which follows, illustrates present-moment living and what it looks like to make the manna paradigm shift and live from manna, not from money. You'll note from her story that even after you make the shift you still have to engage in the practices that create the mindset.

Alone in the Desert

At 75, my friend Margarita sold her home and relocated to Tucson, Arizona. It was a big move to leave the San Francisco Bay Area and move to a town where she had only a handful of acquaintances. She knew that the money from the sale of her home would buy her a cheaper home there, and then she could use the rest to live on.

Like many women these days, Margarita wasn't particularly interested in a full retirement. After she moved, she was able to work remotely for a few months at her job before transitioning out of employment. Then she accepted a freelance project that provided a little income and ordered her day as she resettled into a new routine.

Then the project ended. Her cat died, and then her dog, and she found herself alone in the desert, literally and figuratively.

Margarita had been schooled in powerful spiritual practices in the past and she was a regular meditator. Still, the major transitions, the loss of her work identity and former neighborhood coupled with the loss of her pets and her old routine deeply challenged her faith.

Without a new project to focus on, old survival fears and feelings surfaced. The kind of transition Margarita was going through can cause people to experience back pain (associated with the first chakra) or develop stomach issues (associated with the third chakra). I have often found that when people have issues with money or stability they complain of lower back pain. When people begin to feel a lack of self-confidence or feel helpless they often also start to experience stomach issues.

Margarita shared with me that she could feel energy blocks in her body. She spoke specifically about her chakras and said that the lower energy centers in her body, her root (first), sacral (second), and solar plexus (third) chakras, felt blocked. These three "lower" chakras, which Margarita said she felt were blocked, are associated with survival and safety, abundance and pleasure, and confidence and self-worth.

Margarita continued her daily meditation and spiritual practices. She engaged in consciousness shifting work to elevate her thoughts. She didn't try to change her feelings, she felt her feelings and let them move through her body. She recognized and accepted that these experiences were reflective of an initiation or transition process that she was going through.

She knew she had to get through this initiation. She had to be with this liminal period and surf the waves of discomfort. She knew she had to work through her fears, pivoting from fear to faith.

A few months after her dog died, Margarita decided to get a new dog. Getting a new dog brought something new and joyful into her life. It gave her another purpose. Around that same time, she was offered some freelance work, but the projects didn't feel like a good intuitive fit, so she turned them down—one after the other.

Now you might be thinking: *What? She turned down work? She turned down money?*

Yes. Because Margarita was living by manna. She listened to her intuition, her higher energy centers, her heart (fourth), throat (fifth), third eye (sixth), and crown (seventh) chakras. These chakras are associated with love and inner peace, expressing our truth, seeing the big picture and higher wisdom, and connection to Source itself. She connected to these energies, summoning faith over fear. She wasn't allowing herself to be motivated by fear, which is the opposite of faith. It wasn't that she was being frivolous or foolish. She was listening deeply to her inner guidance and she was clear that declining the projects was the better choice.

After she turned down the third project, a fourth project came to her that was a great fit. In fact, it was an easy freelance project that also supported her in developing a new skill. More specifically, it helped her repurpose a skill she was already great at. This then led to additional freelance work on projects she was excited to be a part of, rather than ones that she felt would have her pulling her hair out.

Margarita's story illustrates how to live by the manna mindset.

Leaving Mitzrayim (Egypt)

You will leave Egypt many times in your life, maybe even in a single day. Every time you turn away from thoughts of lack and limitation, you leave Egypt. Every time you turn from doubt or thoughts of poverty, sickness, failure, you leave Egypt. Every day you choose your freedom, which means you choose to believe in your own ability to align with a greater power within you (God consciousness) to influence your life, you leave Egypt. Freedom is the knowledge that you can influence your destiny, your relationships, how your day unfolds and even how your life unfolds.

The Hebrews wandered in the wilderness for 40 years looking for the Promised Land. How do you survive your "40 years" in the wilderness—the period of gestation of your new life? You breathe. You meditate. You get support. You do affirmative prayer. You use your down time to envision the land of milk and honey. You engage in practices that create the vibrational frequency of the reality that you're creating. You do what's in front of you to do.

This last is what manna is.

Manna is what the Universe shows you to do that day—the actions to take to receive the gifts being offered to you. It's not just about setting intentions and then taking massive action or turning over every stone, as some people believe.

Manna consciousness involves deep listening. It's a deliberate alignment with a consciousness greater than ourselves. Engaging manna consciousness includes the knowledge and faith that when we ask a question, it will be answered at a higher level. We know the solution lies on a different plane than the problem.

When you live from manna consciousness, you stay alert and pay attention to what comes across your desk and arrives in your email account that day. What's the invitation? What is that bit o' manna calling you to do? It may be something easy like making a phone call or writing a follow-up email or dropping something off somewhere or stopping by a coffee shop and bumping into someone and making a new connection or a reconnection. Whatever it is, it will impress itself upon your thoughts a few times. However, if you ignore it, making other things more important, it will go away. That day's manna left uneaten will evaporate.

Embracing the day's actions with alacrity and faith is why it's a paradigm shift. Because most of us hesitate more than this and try to control our outcomes.

Manna consciousness involves staying open and flexible to what life presents us. When we follow the flow, we live with a greater ability to embrace change. Following the flow reorders are priorities. Our lives become less about obligation and more about deep listening to ourselves and to where we are being called to show up.

As opportunities show up in your life, you must have discernment. Does it feel right to you? Are you motivated from joy, fear, greed? Listen deeply to your inner compass. Fear and greed are not aligned with God or manna in the same way that joy or faith is.

Following fear and greed are the very things that threaten to destroy own planet. In fact, it is fear and greed that led to the near extinction of the Indigenous people of the American continent and the destruction of their harmonious way of living with nature and natural law. The Indigenous populations of Turtle Island, as they refer to the American continent, lived by their own version of manna from heaven. They never took more than what they needed. They thanked the Great Spirit every day for what was provided them and they used every part of whatever plant they harvested or animal they killed. Hoarding is antithetical to traditional Native American values. The flowed with the seasons and followed the flow of life, including migrating as needed.

When we begin to sincerely follow the flow, as was and is the way of the Indigenous peoples before Western assimilation, we will begin to live in greater harmony with ourselves and the natural world around us.

Follow the Flow

We can learn to follow the flow. We can follow the breadcrumbs instead of waiting for the whole loaf to come to us, like Jude, one of the participants in my workshops did. Jude was living in Los Angles and working for a start-up tech company when it went belly under. After he lost his job, he and his wife moved to the Inland Empire, a city east of LA and a minimum hour's drive from the ocean, where it was more affordable. He took a job at a bank and they purchased a house they could afford and lived there for many years.

Jude was unhappy though. He was not inspired by his job. He didn't like the Inland Empire. It was too hot and dry for him. He'd gotten caught up, like many of us do, living and working in a way that leaves us dead inside.

Many of us can relate to Jude. We're comfortably uncomfortable. It can seem easier to stay in an unpleasant situation that's familiar, rather than go through the trouble of making changes in our lives such as looking for a new job, packing up all our stuff, selling our home, leaving our friends, and doing something new. And for good reason. Those are huge stressors. Relocation, building your business again or a new community of friends, can be challenging, but it can also come with huge rewards and personal growth if we're willing to try.

Jude had a desire to go north. One day he came home from work and told his wife that he wanted to move to the Pacific Northwest. She agreed and they picked up and moved just like that. Jude didn't know where he would find work, he just knew he had to get out of the desert. They landed in a small coastal town in Washington State.

One thing led to the next and they found a great place to live, and then Jude got a job working for a bookstore. Jude loved the store and he marveled at the amazing view from his "office." He loved his new life and the community that he and his wife were now part of. He was pleased to be surrounded by people who shared his values and, among other things, his love of music, organic gardening, and the great outdoors.

Jude left his proverbial Egypt and relied on manna consciousness. He believed that he could have a better life and he followed the breadcrumbs to his land of milk and honey.

Another client of mine, Shirley, was nearing retirement age, though she knew she didn't want to stop working completely. Shirley sold a property, then rented out her home and relocated to a cheaper city. The money she made on renting out her home covered her mortgage and the rent on her new apartment. At first, she felt stressed by the process, but she hired a property management company that took 10 percent off the profits while dealing with 100 percent of the renter's concerns, repairs, and ultimately stress, so she didn't have to.

Shirley's new apartment was in a walkable area of town that she loved. She'd worked as a language teacher during the school year, then tutored and taught yoga in the summer to supplement her income. After she moved, she got part-time work at the local YMCA and taught Sit and Be Fit classes at the senior center. She also volunteered to teach a weekly French class at the library. She wasn't making as much money as she had when she worked full time as a high school French teacher, but with social security and her rent paid, the extra money she was making paid her bills and for coffee and meals out.

Shirley's new work helped her meet a lot of people and she established herself in the community much more quickly than she would have if she had just stayed home. She was staying active and developed a great community of friends, all of which provided additional social and economic opportunities, including being hired to provide private French lessons. Even more importantly to Shirley, her time was her own. She traveled. She went to workshops when she wanted to. Her life was full.

Alan, another participant in one of my workshops, shared how after one of his jobs ended he felt the desire to learn software coding. He didn't have any experience in this and didn't know where to go for training. Alan knew he needed to get a new job so he opened up the phonebook to look for recruiters, figuring that contacting a recruiting company could help him find his next job. Before there was YELP there was the Yellow Pages. Alan looked up recruiters in the Yellow Pages and called one that caught his eye. The name sounded inspirational. He dialed their number. When they answered he expressed an interest in their recruiting services.

"The phonebook made a mistake," they told him. "We are not a recruiting company."

Alan could have just hung up and moved on to the next name in the phone book. Instead he got curious. "What do you do?" he asked.

"We are a software development company," they told him.

Alan chuckled as he recalled that miraculous moment. "I told them I wanted to learn to code and program software." They responded enthusiastically and told him that they would hire him and train him. "The rest is history," he said. That was the moment Alan begun his over-twenty-year career as a software developer.

The Universe knows the way. We just have to stay open and present and keep following the breadcrumbs.

Stay Present: A Conscious Choice

Manna consciousness is about being aware and present from moment to moment. Our good, our wisdom, our guidance are only available to us in the present. Our job is staying present.

We have no power over the past and the only way to impact our future is utilizing this moment, right now, to its fullest. Staying conscious and present to the thoughts we think and working to actively restore our minds to a place of peace and positive expectancy is the best gift we can give ourselves. Our determination to hold the mental high watch, a new age spiritual term that means expecting the best and seeing the best or highest outcome for any situation, will pay us in dividends. When we consciously choose positive thoughts and self-talk we create an empowered future.

Engage in the practices of this book. Shift your vibrational frequency, act as if, and you'll see that you are in a more positive receptive state of mind available to your manna.

Remember, positivity is a choice. Positivity is a muscle. Positivity is a pivot. Pivot again and again to get yourself back in the flow.

THIRTEEN

ෆ౨

OPEN YOUR HEART

The heart is the path to liberation and freedom. If you
want to truly be free from the world's mental
entrapment you need to listen to your inner compass:
your heart.

One of the fundamentals of getting into and staying in
the manna mindset is opening your heart. An open heart
brings clarity, optimism, and flexibility. An open heart is
powerful. A person who has an open heart is available to
life and aware of the currents of energy moving around
them. A person with an open heart is also available to
listen to their own inner stirrings.

Listen to your Heart

In my book *It's Never Too Late to Be Your Self,* I shared
about the importance of following your heart and living
a life in which your heart leads. I shared a process I call
hearticulation that includes quieting the mind, opening
your heart, connecting with the power of love, which
creates a flow state, and then tapping into your heart's
desires.

Listening to your heart's desires will change your life.

As discussed, the mind and its distorted thinking is the place of our enslavement. Our minds can be brainwashed, but we don't have this equivalent with the heart. We don't have heart control, only mind control. The heart is the path to liberation and freedom. If you want to truly be free from the world's mental entrapment you need to listen to your inner compass—your heart. Connect with your feelings first, then let your mind follow.

Your heart, not your head, ought to guide important decisions in your life, such as your marriage partner, career path, home, family, and even finances. Most of us learned from our education and family systems to prioritize logic. We were taught to believe that following our hearts is foolish. Yet success that comes at the expense of our happiness is empty success.

This doesn't mean you throw out logic, but the heart should lead the mind, not the other way around. When you let your heart lead you will create a far healthier physiological state in your body. It's not possible to have a joyful life if you are disconnected from your heart.

Like I said before, listening to your heart is a lifestyle change, it will reorder your life. It may disrupt your life in the short term, but in the long term it will be worth it. When you live from your heart, you slow down and begin living your life in alignment with your true essence. There will be less resistance and greater flow in all that you do and all that you endeavor to do.

Athletes describe the flow state as *being in the zone;* this is a state of mind in which a person is fully immersed in an activity, they have a sense of energized focus, and the activity they are engaged in occurs effortlessly.

The HeartMath Institute, which studies the relationship between the heart and the brain, has a term for that flow state, anchored in love. They call it *coherence.*

Coherence

Coherence is the "state when the heart, mind, and emotions are in energetic alignment and cooperation."[1] Like manna consciousness, it is an elevated state of consciousness. The HeartMath Institute reports that this alignment, which they call *physiological coherence,* creates increased synchronization and harmony between the cognitive, emotional, and physiological systems, resulting in efficient and harmonious functioning of the whole" and that it results in a "substantial improvement in cognitive function such as long- and short-term memory, increased ability to focus and process information and an overall improvement in learning."[2]

Additionally, they report that when someone is in the state of coherence they experience an elevated positive state of mind and that this has mental health benefits, including an increase in resilience that allows them to "effectively manage stressful situations and recover from them more quickly" without a decline in energy.[3]

Put simply, when you are feeling loving, your brain and body are functioning at an optimal level. You can think clearly, and this feels good in your body.

When you're feeling unloving, by contrast, you create stress in your mind and body, and this negatively impacts your well-being.

Coherence can be measured on an EKG or ECG machine that records heart-rate variability (HRV), the time between your heartbeats.[4]

Low HRV means that the intervals between your heartbeats are constant, thus you have a low variability. High HRV means that the intervals between your heartbeats are more irregular and less consistent.

In the case of coherence, variability is our desired outcome. High HRV is associated with greater coherence.[5] Perhaps think of it in this way, it is healthier to have more spontaneity between heart beats than for your heart beats to be stuck in the same old rut.

High HRV is different from an arrhythmia in which the rate of the rhythm of your heartbeat is either too fast (tachycardia) or too slow (bradycardia), or irregular (dysrhythmia or atrial fibrillation). High HRV may also be associated with physical fitness, a healthy heart, and the ability to roll with the proverbial punches.[6]

A low HRV suggests less resilience to stress and is associated with disease and higher mortality rates.[7] When we're younger we have more variability (high HRV) and as we get older we have less variability between heart beats (low HRV).

HRV is controlled by our autonomic nervous systems (ANS), which includes the functions of both the parasympathetic and the sympathetic nervous systems, the rest-and-digest and fight-or-flight nervous systems. HRV relates to our breathing, heart rate, blood pressure, and digestion because the ANS regulates all of these functions.[8] Measuring our HRV allows us to assess imbalances in the ANS.

Low HRV is associated with increased stress and an overactive fight-or-flight response.[9] It's important to note that when we are in fight or flight our body emits the stress hormones adrenaline and cortisol into the bloodstream, this causes our bodies to temporarily shut off nonessential systems and focus on addressing the threat at hand.

This response is obviously positive, as it helps us survive. However, if we are in a constant state of stress, our bodies are continuously flooded by cortisol and we are at an increased risk for mental and physical health problems.[10]

The HeartMath Institute asserts that when we are in coherence and we are in the state of feeling love our bodies emit hormones into the bloodstream, like DHEA and oxytocin.[11] According to McCraty and Zayas (2014), "The nature of the emotional experience appears to be related to the level of coherence of the heart rhythm pattern. Emotions typically thought of as positive, such as appreciation and compassion, are related to a more coherent heart rhythm pattern; whereas emotions that are typically thought of as negative are related to more

Heart Rhythms (Heart Rate Variability)

Image courtesy of the HeartMath® Institute: www.heartmath.org.

incoherent pattern, suggesting that positive emotions may have a renewing physiological effect and negative emotions may have a depleting physiological effect."[12]

Put simply, when we are experiencing emotions like love, gratitude, appreciation and joy, this has a positive impact on our mental and physical functioning. When we experience emotions like rage, disgust, envy, jealousy, and sadness, this saps us of our life force, draining our mental and physical energy. Of course, over time this can contribute to disease and premature aging.

According to the HeartMath Institute emotional distress is visible in the HRV waveforms, specifically "emotional stress—including emotions such as anger, frustration, and anxiety—gives rise to heart rhythm patterns that appear irregular and erratic: the HRV waveform looks like a series of uneven, jagged peaks."[13]

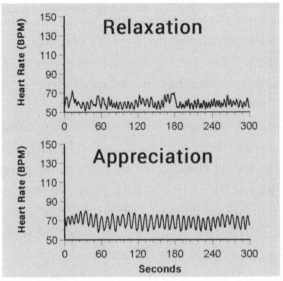

Image courtesy of the HeartMath®
Institute: www.heartmath.org.

These jagged waveforms are known as "incoherent heart rhythm pattern."[14]

The HeartMath Institute asserts that while relaxation and anything that helps us calm the mind creates positive results in our lives, waves produced when in a state of relaxation (as compared to those produced when a subject is in a feeling state of appreciation and gratitude) differ significantly.

While both states create a rhythmic wave pattern, the state of relaxation creates a rhythmic pattern that is more spiked, while the waves associated with coherence are rounded–more like gumdrops.[17] Relaxation lowers the heart rate and is associated with an increase in the functions of the rest and digest nervous system.

Coherence does not lower the heart rate; coherence changes the rhythm of the wave.[18] Coherence creates a fluid wave.

Therefore, coherence is different than relaxation because we remain in an alert state.

Opening your heart will allow you to get into that state of positive expectancy and coherence. Manna consciousness is empowered by heart-brain coherence. When we are in a state of coherence, we have greater expression of our creative abilities and the capacity to tune in to frequencies beyond our material world and receive more orderly coherent streams of consciousness and energy. This is why it is essential for us to make sure we are feeling emotions like gratitude, love, and appreciation to create and regularly experience the state of coherence in our bodies.

Love is powerful and good for your health.[19] I invite you to focus on creating a state of love within yourself and do what you can to sustain it. When you are able to remain in a state of love it will shift everything. Meditation without love is not enough. Meditation creates relaxation. Love shifts reality.

How Do Open Your Heart?

It's important for you to discover what uniquely works for you to open your heart and feel love. Perhaps it's thinking about someone in your life you feel affection for such as a pet, your children or grandchildren, a good friend, a sweetheart or spouse. Someone who, when you think about them, you feel delight. Thinking about who you love and allowing yourself to feel that love for them will help you open your heart. This is a great place to start. You can spend time thinking about them, bringing back an image of them in your mind and reliving good memories.

Better yet, you can make sure you're spending time with the people you love. It's important to pet and snuggle with your animal companions, play with your children (grandchildren, nieces, nephews), enjoy a meal, a cup of coffee, a talk, or a walk with your friends, siblings, sweethearts. It's important to make time for the people who matter to you.

It's also important to go to places you love. For many of us, that is nature. Going to the beach or a drive in the country can open your heart. Anywhere you can surround yourself in beauty. The heart loves that. If flowers open your heart bring some home or plant them in a flower box or your yard. If plants make you happy get some. If being in nature makes you happy find a way to bring more nature into your life. Even if it's just walking to the nearest park or eating your sandwich there, do it. Just get some time with greenspace. Kick off your shoes and let your bare feet touch earth.

As I discussed in my book *It's Never Too Late to Be Your Self,* keeping your mind and home clutter free will help you stay connected to your heart. Only hold on to the things that bring you joy, as this will transform how you feel. This includes your thoughts. We spend an inordinate amount of time thinking about what pisses us off. We let too many things get stuck in our craws and we're unwilling to just let those thoughts go.

What if we spent more time thinking loving thoughts, thinking about what brings us joy? What if we looked around and noticed all the joyful things in our immediate vicinity? What if we spent time appreciating what's around us?

As I write this, I can appreciate the beautiful plants in the colorful pots on the windowsill, the delicious cup of frothy coffee I'm enjoying, the attractive architecture of the building I'm in, the comfortable clothes I'm wearing, and the view outside of the beautiful blue sky and spectacular fluffy clouds swirling above.

What can you appreciate around you right now? What if instead of dredging up your resentments, you delighted in the little details of life and the bigger things you seem to take for granted? Imagine how that focus would allow you to keep your heart open and move from one activity to another with a joyful heart.

Meditation will help you relax and keep your heart open. Take some time to meditate and to declutter your mind. Focus on what you're grateful for and express and feel appreciation for all the good in your life. This will help you get into and stay in a receptive and open-hearted space.

Mini-Hearticulation Meditation

Use the following meditation to help you open your heart. Practice it as many times as needed until it becomes easy for you to connect with love every day.

Take a deep breath and close your eyes. Bring your focus to the present moment.

Take another breath and let your body relax.

Pause and reflect on what you're grateful for.

Your breath? Your body? Loved ones?

Let in the gratitude.

Remember you live in a friendly universe.

Good. Now, what are you holding on to that you need to release?

A grudge? A to-do list? Self-doubt?

Just let it go. Surrender it.

Breathe and relax even more deeply.

Now begin to breathe into your heart chakra. Relaxing the muscles around the heart. Softening.

Good. Take another deep breath in. Keep letting go as you exhale.

Now gently allow yourself to remember a time when you felt deep love. Let that feeling wash over you.

It could have been love for an animal companion, a friend, a sweetheart, family member or child.

Allow that love to awaken your heart and soften it. Amplify that feeling.

Keep breathing and relaxing your body.

Good now, remember a time when you felt deep reverence for a sunset or nature.

Anchor into that.

Remember a time when you felt a deep love for life itself.

Good now feel that love and imagine you're walking on the beach, sitting by a river or stream, watching the sun rise, and set.

Now begin to feel the Oneness of all life.

Allow yourself to feel it. Unity. No Separation.

Good. And feel all of life loving you. Surrounding you with love and peace.

Now as your heart opens even more, ask yourself:

- What is my heart yearning for?
- What would bring me joy?
- How can I be a loving presence in the world?

Just allow whatever wants to emerge to come to you.

What does that feel like it? What does it look like? Feel it in your body.

FOURTEEN

∽

REST AND PLAY

*Real abundance is: Choice. Freedom. Space to be with
your own thoughts and make your own decisions.*

Sometimes when you find yourself struggling yet
getting nowhere, or feeling the pointlessness of life, it's
time to simply give it a rest. Sometimes the best action
is to do nothing. Well, not exactly nothing. Sometimes
we need to take a break from all goal-directed action. In
other words, we need to rest and play.

We've already discussed that when you find yourself
in the energy of efforting—trying to force a positive or
particular outcome by continuing to work hard yet
achieving undesirable and unsuccessful results—
surrendering may be the best option.

We've also discussed the importance of staying
present and following the flow, waiting until there is
clarity on what action to take next.

It is essential to make time for the nourishment that
comes from recreation and fun. Intentionally creating
space and time for nonproductive activity enhances our
mood and our feelings of well-being and inner
prosperity. We need time to *recreate.* If you break the

157

word down it is to re-create. We are creating ourselves again. We are enjoying our existence.

Play involves fun. Having fun makes us smile and laugh and feel joy. And just as opening our hearts does, playing relaxes us and is a buffer against stress and stress chemicals in our body.

For some, the idea of being unproductive will bring up anxiety. Some of us don't know how to play. Or even relax. Having nothing to do or doing nothing can be emotionally triggering. Many people get so focused on accomplishing things on their to do lists, whether or not they are urgent or important, that the idea of relaxing or slowing down launches them into an emotional tailspin. All the emotions they've been out-running may catch up with them—all those feelings they've kept at bay through frenzied action or their daily grind. Like when I was in graduate school and would get sick every spring and Christmas vacation because that's when my adrenalized body could finally crash and get some rest.

If you have trouble with the idea of pausing the action and taking a break, you're not alone. Many in industrialized countries have a hard time giving it a rest. We've been conditioned this way. We value ourselves and others for our net worth and ability to produce.

On the Seventh Day . . .

One of the covenants that the ancient Hebrews made with God was to observe the sabbath. When they were slaves in Egypt, they could not take a day off from laboring. They were forced to work or else be physically beaten. Once they were free, they could observe sabbath. Observing the sabbath for Jews and Christians means working six days and taking the seventh day off. For Jews, the sabbath is Saturday.

For observant Jews and Seventh Day Adventists, all work stops at sunset on Friday and families gather together to enjoy time doing nonwork-related activities, including spiritual study. No money is exchanged, and no fires are lit. The idea is that even the primary cook for the family gets a day off. Meals are prepped ahead of time so that everyone can rest.

While Christians also embrace the idea of Sunday as a day of worship and many businesses are closed, in today's modern world, commerce takes place seven days a week and many people are expected to work one way or another, seven days a week, and the boundary between work and rest is blurred.

With the creation of cellphones and email came the expectation from many employers that we be available to work 24/7. This is especially prevalent now that we are being forced into remote working by the threat of the coronavirus. Whereas previously people had some clear distinctions between home and the workplace, the workplace now follows them wherever their phone goes.

Our digital technology and poorly communicated social boundaries have tethered us even more strongly to our employers and their expectations of us.

This is another form of Pharaoh's enslavement. It's also just plain rude.

You need to insist on taking time off. Taking a day off creates space between you and the external world. You come back to yourself. You realize that the world outside of you is a construction.

You separate yourself from the profane by making time for the sacred. You draw a line in the sand, a distinction, between Pharaoh's world (the world of humankind) and God's world (the Divine).

You can't create something new when you're stuck in the grind. You need to be able to step back and detox from the work world and attune to your own voice, your own truth. You can't feel or imagine something bigger or better for yourself when you're working 24/7. You're caught in the hamster wheel. You need to be able to get off and reflect.

Rest Will Help You Reset into Manna Consciousness

Thoughts create our reality. When we are caught up in the drudgery of life, our thoughts remain in low vibration. Low-vibration thoughts and feelings keep us from attaining manna consciousness. If we've fallen out of manna consciousness, we need to be able to reset. We need to take a break from the world. We need to turn off the news, noise and chaos. Thus, the power of the Sabbath.

The seventh day of the week is the day of rest when we turn our attention back to Source. We turn off the lights of the outside world and tune in to the inner light. We seek the wisdom of the Divine over the ways of the world. This allows us to stay connected to our true Source. Our true Source is not humankind. Our true Source is not Pharaoh. We do not toil for Pharaoh. We remember that we are Divine beings here on purpose with the purpose to evolve spiritually.

Ultimately, our purpose is love. It is not destruction of the planet. It is not material consumption. It is not to gorge ourselves in physical pleasure with drugs and sex. It is to live harmoniously. It is to remember our oneness with all of life.

On your day of rest, do things that inspire you, fill you up, and nourish your soul. Take a beach day or go for a drive in the country. Go to the movies or have lunch with a friend. Find a way to have fun, to stay light and open. When we are open and light, it keeps us from freaking out and becoming overwhelmed with rigidity and fear. You can't do both things at the same time.

The pharaohs of the world would like us to be fearful, as this gives them power. When we are afraid, we are not available to the magic and power of manna consciousness. We are more controllable. When we are in fear we are more competitive, less cooperative. When we are in fear we are subject to small mindedness. We are subject to racism and xenophobia and repel our good. We close our hearts.

Working Nine to Five

Before COVID 19, in the United States where I live people had longer workdays than other western countries. While France customarily has a 35-hour workweek, Italy a 39-hour workweek, and the Netherlands a 29-hour workweek, in the United States our perspective is that the average workweek is 40 hours. That's a typical nine-to-five schedule Monday through Friday. But our practice is to work even longer and some Americans are working more than one job to make ends meet.

According to a 2014 Gallup poll, most Americans actually worked 47 hours a week and 40 percent reported working more than 50 hours per week.[1] That means the average American spends eight more hours at work per week than the average Italian (that's an additional workday), 12 more hours than the French citizen (one and a half days more at work), and 18 more hours than the Dutch citizen which is half their workweek. That's why they have time for cappuccinos and gourmet home cooking.

And this is just the *average* American. As mentioned above, some American workers are spending more than 50 hours a week on the job and/or responding to work requests on texts and emails, something several European Union countries have banned after hours.

My client, Theresa, was working 60 hours a week. She worked at the office from nine to six, then commuted an hour each way and when she returned home she worked on her computer after her children went to sleep. She had very limited time to spend with her family. Another client, James, commuted to Google in Mountain View, California, from Salinas, California, 74 miles away where he could afford to buy a home. James spent two hours in the car every morning and every evening to get to and from his office.

You Need a Vacation

Vacation is equally as important as a day of rest because vacation allows you to feel free. You feel the vibration of freedom in your body. You begin to notice what it's like to find your own pace, your own rhythm. You make choices based on your desires, not on your employers or routine. You're fresh. This is what real abundance is. Choice. Freedom. Space to be with your own thoughts and make your own decisions.

If you travel, you are also exposed to new ideas, new ways of living. This perspective can be liberating. I remember when I went to Italy and noticed there were no to-go cups and people took time to enjoy their coffees while chatting with one another.

Having space and time creates a feeling of abundance and allows you to connect with your higher self and shift your frequency. When we have the space and time to connect with our authentic selves and desires we begin to activate a new frequency and this new frequency opens us up to new possibilities in our lives.

Americans not only work more hours weekly, they enjoy fewer vacation days than other western countries. The United Kingdom gives their people 28 mandatory paid vacation days; Denmark, Finland, Norway, and Sweden, 25 paid vacation days. Additionally, the European Union requires all member countries to provide at least 20 paid vacation days.

The typical worker at a U.S. company gets only ten paid days off. Many people are afraid to take their vacation days because they don't want to get behind on their work or they worry that others will see them as less serious about their jobs.

The United States has become more and more divided into two classes: a worker/servant class and an owner/master class. People are afraid to care for themselves for fear that they will lose their jobs. This is a part of our mental enslavement.

Our long workhours contribute to feelings of loneliness. They also contribute to feeling less compassion for ourselves and others. This mentality is created because we are rushing around focused on survival needs. We don't have time to play. We become more serious, less creative. The system treats us like machines and then we expect that from ourselves and others. We deny our own and other's humanity. We become more focused on survival and seeing our livelihood coming from outside of ourselves. We see others as threats to our well-being. We begin to commodify the earth because we don't have time to enjoy natural places. We become angry with people who have access to resources we now perceive as precious. We become more tribal and territorial. We can see the impact of this on our daily news.

Power to the People

We need to say no to working 24/7 and forgoing our vacation days. We can no longer be enslaved to the corporations and the almighty dollar. We need to take back our power.

It's like the proverbial frog in a pot of water. Someone once wrote that if you put a frog in a pot of boiling water it will jump out, but if you put it in and slowly turn up the heat it will stay until it's cooked. I don't think this is true, but the point is clear. That's what happens for many of us in bad relationships. That's what has happened to the workers in the U.S. We've become habituated to allowing our employers to demand more and more from us in exchange for less and less compensation.

Imagine what could be possible if we prioritized our lives and demanded companies respond to our needs, not the other way around. We need to stop being complicit in our mental enslavement. We can't let corporate culture shape our values. We need to prioritize people over profits, humanity over greed.

Decide what your values are: health, family, quality of life? Don't let others tell you that achievement, ladder climbing, and working long hours and overtime are the only or most important qualities. Don't let anyone define your worth by your net-worth or your status.

Trust that if you set the limits and decide you will no longer be exploited, the Universe will respond. People might also respect you more if you set better boundaries for yourself.

Take a Break

According to a 2017 *Harvard Business Review* article, "To Be More Creative, Schedule Your Breaks," people who take regular breaks demonstrate more creative thinking. The article states, "When you're working on tasks that would benefit from creative thinking, consciously insert breaks to refresh your approach. Set them at regular intervals—use a timer if you have to."[2] The article reported that people who did this came up with more novel solutions to problems than people who persisted at a task. This is likely why many writers and writing coaches encourage people who have writers block to take a break when they're feeling stuck, and do things like going for a walk, painting, taking a shower, or even shelving a project in a drawer for a month to get some perspective again.

My friend Philip, who is a professional screenwriter, can attest to the efficacy of this strategy. Philip shares that when he is unable to write or feels stuck with a plot point he will close his laptop and go for a walk or take a nap or sit quietly and pet his cat. Taking a break from his writing allows him to relax and let creative ideas flow again.

Taking a break is good for your mind and your body too. For example, when you've been engaging in high-intensity exercise, it's good to follow that up with active and passive recovery. *Active recovery* includes engaging in low-intensity activities, such as yoga and walking, while *passive recovery* involves resting. According to *Healthline* magazine, active recovery can help you stay flexible, eliminate toxins, reduce soreness, and increase blood flow.[3] However, when you've overexerted yourself or injured yourself taking a full day of rest is the best course of action.

All this is to say, that far from doing *nothing*, rest and recovery is the *something* that one can do. Resting and playing will help you stay in manna consciousness. This means that when you are "doing nothing" you're actually engaged in the art of recovery. You're practicing recovery. This may be especially helpful for those who struggle with workaholism or who would identify themselves as having type-A personalities.

Remember, you are not doing *nothing*. You are "doing" the resting.

Just Be

When we are caught up in being "productive," "accomplishing things," and "climbing the ladder," we begin to feel that our worth is related to our net worth and our status. Many people find that when they get the promotion, the house, the car, the spouse and two kids, and the picket fence, they begin asking, *Is this all there is?* They ask this question because they've been trying to meet the ego's needs, but the ego is insatiable and driven by fear. It cannot be satisfied, only calmed or stilled.

Happiness is an inside job. *Doing* does not bring peace. *Being* does. We have a right to just be. We don't have to justify our existence with activity, accomplishment and status. True joy and peace lie within.

Embrace doing nothing. Sitting on the beach. Walking in nature. Laying in a field. Sitting on the porch. These activities will allow you to connect with your essential self. When you connect with your essential self, you are sovereign. You are available to manna consciousness. You are available to divine grace.

I'm not saying do this every day or all the time. Then you would be wasting your creative abilities and missing your opportunities to contribute and have meaning and purpose in your life. However, make it a weekly practice to take a whole day or afternoon off to just be and know yourself as a human being, not just a "human doing." This will allow you to experience the sweetness of life. This will make your life feel rich.

What Happened When People Took a Vacation or Time Off

When I took three weeks off on a trip to Italy, I realized how much I disliked my work environment. When I returned I quit my job and started my own private practice.

Since the COVID-19 pandemic began, many people have realized that they don't want to work as hard as before and have enjoyed not having a commute. Some people have begun to advocate for four-day workweeks—three-day weekends! I was proposing something similar when I began writing this book.

Several friends and colleagues have shared with me that they never want to go back to their old lives. For one thing, they say they don't miss their commutes or their long hours at work. Other folks said they appreciated having more time to be intentional about their meal planning and quality time spent with family. Several felt that they were living more according to the natural rhythms and felt they had more time to be creative, meditate, and had more energy.

My client Sandra, a holistic practitioner, has realized that she was paying too much rent for her office space and decided that she preferred to work part time. She found that by having more time to herself and quality time with her husband made her happier. She moved her practice to a shared office space that was cheaper, which also meant she didn't have to work as many hours to pay her overhead.

A couple I was working with found that with more time on their hands and less money coming in, they really preferred to live closer to nature. They left their expensive rental in the city and moved several states away to a rural area where they could have land and a garden. Their kids were thrilled too. My clients realized that they could choose the way they wanted to educate their kids and delighted in the fact that they could now offer them lessons on flexibility and self-sufficiency.

Another client of mine, Ananya, began working from home during the COVID-19 pandemic. Ananya told me she didn't like her job and felt that she was killing time by being there. She decided to enroll in online classes in homeopathy, something she'd always been interested in and had never had time to pursue because of a long commute and a demanding tech job. She loved the classes so much that she decided to go back to school full time so she could make a career change.

Time Off: A Self-Reflection

What happened for you if/when you had to take time off during the COVID-19 pandemic?
Were there other times you had to take time off?
What did you do?
How did it change you?

PART THREE

❦

EMBODY MANNA CONSCIOUSNESS

The two chapters in Part Three focus on embodying manna consciousness on a daily basis. They will teach you how to actively make the manna paradigm shift. This is where the proverbial rubber meets the road. This is where you go from reading a book to transforming your life.

FIFTEEN

ରଡ

MAKE THE MANNA
PARADIGM SHIFT

Free your mind and the manna will follow.

As you go through the manna paradigm shift, go slowly. Allow yourself to engage in all the fundamental practices and, like a snowball gathering snow, your manna consciousness will grow. Like establishing spokes of the wheel, the more spokes you have on the wheel, the better it will turn. You want all the spokes working together.

Each fundamental skill you've developed ultimately will help you embody manna consciousness and stay in a manna mindset on a daily basis.

Never forget, you choose your reality here. You determine your experience, setting the stakes, based on how deeply you engage in these practices.

Let's review.

Opening the Door to Manna Consciousness

We have two parts of our autonomic nervous system, the sympathetic and the parasympathetic. The sympathetic nervous system is also called the fight-or-flight nervous system.

Our fight-or-flight response gets us into action. When we are in this state, our breathing is shallow and our heart rate rapid. Fight-or-flight is the state of fear. Our bodies perceive that we are in danger. We are on high alert. The fight-or-flight signal tells us that we should be alert.

The parasympathetic nervous system regulates the opposite response as stress. It is also known as the rest-and-digest nervous system. Here's the mnemonic I learned in grad school to remember the difference. If you have a parachute on a plane, you can kick back and relax and enjoy eating your snacks on the flight.

Parasympathetic = parachute = rest and digest.

When our parasympathetic nervous system is in control, we are calm and relaxed.

The two nervous systems cannot operate simultaneously. Therefore, if we want to override our stress response and activate the relaxation response, we can take deep, relaxing breaths. We focus on slowing down our heart rate.

By having an intentional practice, like meditation, we begin our day from a place of inner calm. Making time for meditation, whether it's 4 or 40 minutes, and taking deep, relaxed breaths will communicate to your nervous system that all is well.

We must be intentional with this. As we engage in deep breathing we create calm and openness which facilitates the receptive state of manna consciousness.

When we feel good about ourselves and our lives, we breathe more deeply. When we feel safe and secure, our bodies are relaxed.

Manna consciousness is embodied with deep breathing, relaxation and positive expectancy. We can set the tone of our day by creating a sense of peace, positive expectancy, and confidence in our bodies.

Your embodiment of manna consciousness will be palpable to others. They will feel more comfortable in your presence. They will feel as if your confidence your positive expectancy has a magnetic pull and it will activate more opportunities for you. Additionally, when you assume the physiology of relaxation and expansion, you won't be contracting your energy and it will be easier for you to keep holding the frequency of your good manifested.

This is what I was trying to share with Lucinda, who owns an antique shop down the street from one of the cafes I write in. I went into Lucinda's store for the first time during the period I was writing this book. I'd passed the store many times, but it always seemed closed.

"How are you?" I greeted the woman behind the counter.

"I'm okay," Lucinda said halfheartedly. I immediately sensed she'd been crying, and she wasn't going to put on an act.

One of the things about being a psychologist is that it's hard to walk away from human suffering. People frequently tell me their problems and sometimes I just can't help but ask. Within moments, Lucinda was sharing with me that her mother had died after being sick for a long time and that on most days she could barely get herself to the store. Her inability to open the store meant that she wasn't making any money, which meant that she was having trouble paying her bills.

"I don't know what's wrong with me," Lucinda said.

"You're grieving," I replied.

"But it was going on before my mom died."

"Your mom was sick for a long time. That's likely when your grieving started. You're depressed and need support."

"I feel like I'm not going to make any money and I'm going to lose everything. My mind is racing with thoughts about my failure and everything that could go wrong."

"You've just lost a lot," I said. "And you might lose your business." I sympathized. "May I share something with you?" I asked.

She nodded.

"You are more likely to lose your business if you keep thinking thoughts about your failure. I know you know this. You've got to start shifting your thoughts. When those negative thoughts come up you have to pivot them to something better. If you could muster up some faith and lean into the Universe for support, your situation could improve. Your job is to just get up in the morning and get yourself here."

"You're right," she said. "I know that. Things have worked out before."

"Keep showing up," I said. "Keep your open sign up." She smiled and thanked me.

Keeping our door open and our energetic sign on is an important part of manna consciousness. We need to keep doing the work to stay open and receptive.

Other Ways to Embody Manna Consciousness

How do we get into the manna mindset and embody manna consciousness? How do we go from the place Lucinda was in, where we can't stop ruminating about our failures and thinking about worst-case scenarios?

As I discussed in chapter 4, "Break Your Mental Chains," we can start by recognizing the thinking errors when they show up and remember that those are negative tricks the mind is playing on us. Those thoughts are not true, nor are they reality. We have to stay focused on the present moment. We remind ourselves, *I am safe in this moment.* We do what's in front of us to do.

With Lucinda, I said, "If you have to close the store or lose the business you'll deal with that then. You're not there now. Stay focused on the present."

Here are some tactics you can use to stay in manna consciousness. You can:

Shift your thoughts. Focus on what you want to happen. Tell yourself, *I can do this. I am connected to a source greater than myself that knows how to do it, even if I don't.*

Edit out bad news. Choosing to be intentional about what you're listening to or what you're consuming mentally will help you stay in manna consciousness. Don't turn on the news first thing in the morning. If you don't have to, don't turn it on at all. If you do watch it or hear it, put it into perspective. Let it inform you, but don't let it take you down. Make a mental note of what's happening while at the same time making a conscious choice not to continue to dwell on it or rehash it with others.

Get physical. Physical movement will help you get out of your head and the defeated, depressed physiology that people often embody when they are depressed or desperate.

Go for walks. Walking helps you connect with a steady rhythm in your body.

Exercise. Go for a run, lift weights, do yoga. Get into your body. Feel your strength and flexibility.

Dance. Dancing creates joy in your body. Shake that thing. *Mueve las caderas!* Create that Joy Jams play list I mentioned previously.

Surround yourself with beauty. Go forest-bathing, walk through a rose garden, sit by the ocean. Give your eyes something beautiful to rest upon. Inspiring views and nature are delightful to the eyes and uplift us.

Surround yourself with good scents. Purchase some essential oils. Lavender. Rose. Jasmine. Earthy smells. Pine needles. Fresh-cut grass. Even chimney smoke would work if it helps you relax.

Live from your heart. Align your mind with your heart. You don't want to move through the day led by your head, driven by fear and worry. You want your heart to lead. You want your day to flow from the soft places of your heart, not from the pressures in your head. If you're worrying that your heart is informing you about a "deep-state cabal" or other conspiracy theories, that is not your heart. Your heart may urge you to get involved and take action to improve a situation, but your heart wouldn't indulge you in conspiracy theories; that's your head. Fear is created in the mind and felt in the gut.

The gut, not the heart, deals in fear. Fear is reactionary. It may or may not be logical. Homophobia and xenophobia are illogical, fear-based reactions. Someone may have a homophobic fear that they believe is "gut" based. That supposed "gut feeling" comes from being taught to fear LGBT people or people who are different than them.

The heart is about love and openness. The heart deals in kindness and compassion. Your heart draws you lovingly in the direction of something. You can tell it's your heart because it will come from joy, not righteousness.

When your heart is open and you feel more at home in your body, and more at peace in your life, you will increase your ability to embody manna consciousness.

Are Your Thoughts Creating Manna Consciousness? Self-Reflection

Take a look at your thoughts by keeping a thought journal for a day or a week. Notice what you've been focused on.

Are you ruminating about your fears, your bills, your health?

Do you spend time thinking about fun and relaxing vacations, having great sex with your partner, and enjoying good times with friends and family?

Do you imagine yourself succeeding at whatever endeavor you're engaged in, whether it's parenting or making a delicious meal for your family, getting a high mark on a test or negotiating a successful deal, or getting a great price for the purchase or sale of your home?

What topic or topics do you spend the majority of your mental energy focusing on?

Would you say that your thoughts land more in the "life is working out for me" realm or the "life sucks and then you die" realm?

SIXTEEN

෯

THE 30-DAY MANNA CHALLENGE

We are at the threshold in every moment. We can choose bondage, or we can choose to freely live our lives.

Making the manna paradigm shift is not something you do once and then forget. It is an ongoing daily practice, a moment-by-moment choice to live from manna, not from man. I know it can be done and I know it can change your life, because I've done it and I've witnessed other people doing it again and again. That's the power of the Universe.

Shifting your mindset to one of absolute trust in the beneficence of the Universe is not easy. It requires letting go of your fear. Releasing fear is simple, but it's not about inaction. You don't just sit back and do nothing.

You must engage in the practices. You must do the work to shift your consciousness into manna consciousness. You can't be bitter and skeptical and open and receptive at the same time. You can't sit idly by. You must meditate. You must shift your thinking from simply wishful thinking to conscious, expectant, miracle-minded thinking—and, as I have tried to share with you in the book, *there is a difference.*

I've provided a 30-Day Manna Challenge to help you actively engage in the process of creating a manna mindset. I've also created some online programs to help you make the manna paradigm shift that you can find on my website (see Resources). Are you ready to make the Manna Paradigm Shift?

How the Challenge Works

For the next 30 days, you will shift from living by money to living by manna. Your focus will be on creating inner prosperity, trusting life and living by manna consciousness.

Doing the 30-Day Manna Challenge will help you connect with your own creative power. Every day, you will set the conscious intention of choosing your freedom over bondage to outside circumstances and the world of appearances. Every day, you will energize your connection to Source.

When you engage in the 30-Day Manna Challenge you'll see your manna comes not from the Pharaohs of the world, but from your Source.

In order to make the manna paradigm shift, you will:

- Choose freedom every day.
- Turn away from mental enslavement.
- Connect with a source greater than yourself.
- Speak affirmations. (See "The Nine Fundamental Affirmations" on page 199)

STEP 1: CHOOSE FREEDOM

Day 1–2 Choose Freedom

To begin, in a journal, write down what conditions or situations you feel challenged by.

Next, choose freedom by speaking the Manna Mindset Manifesto:

"I choose freedom. I am a sovereign being, free from enslavement. I have a direct connection with the Source of all life. The Universe is my source and sufficiency in all things. All of my needs are met by the Universe in perfect timing. I receive manna from heaven daily and I am grateful."

You'll be using this mantra every day for the rest of the Challenge.

STEP 2: TURN AWAY FROM YOUR MENTAL ENSLAVEMENT

Day 3–4 Turn Away from Mental Enslavement

Choose freedom by speaking the Manna Mindset Manifesto (see "Days 1–2").

Throughout the day, witness your thoughts. Observe how often you have thoughts like: *How will I pay my bills? I don't have enough money. I can't afford this.*

Remind yourself, *All of my needs are met by the Universe.* You are not denying the situation, you are shifting your focus to possibility and from the place of possibility, not desperation, your needs will be met.

At the end of the day, take out your journal and notice if you've had any unloving thoughts come up, any attack thoughts against yourself, or any cognitive distortions. Answer the following questions: *Is this thought true? If this thought is not true-what else might be true? Is this thought a cognitive error? If so, which one? If this thought were true how would I handle it?*

This is the process discussed in chapter 4, "Break Your Mental Chains."

STEP 3: CONNECT WITH A SOURCE GREATER THAN YOURSELF

Day 5–6 Connect with a Source Greater Than Yourself

Choose freedom by speaking the Manna Mindset Manifesto (see "Days 1–2").

Meditate for five minutes.

Write down any negative self-talk you experience during the day. Review at the end of the day. Reread chapter 4 to refer to how to deal with cognitive distortions.

Day 7 Rest and Relax

STEP 4: CREATE THE MANNA MINDSET BY
SPEAKING THE NINE FUNDAMENTAL
AFFIRMATIONS

Day 8–9 Surrender

Choose freedom by speaking the Manna Mindset Manifesto (see "Days 1–2").

Meditate for ten minutes.

Keep a journal of negative self-talk, and now respond to those thoughts as if you were your own therapist/best friend at the end of the day.

Throughout the day, you will soften and let go. You will allow yourself to be mentally and emotionally receptive by stating the affirmation for surrender: "I am open to the Universe to bring forth my answers."

Day 10–11 Clear Your Mind and Create a New Vision

Choose freedom by speaking the Manna Mindset Manifesto (see "Days 1–2").

Meditate for 15 minutes then do the "A New Vision for Your Life Meditation." You will find a YouTube video guiding you through the meditation on my YouTube channel (see Resources).

Review your answers from the "New Vision for Your Life" exercise in chapter 8.

End your day by stating the affirmation for a new vision:

"I allow a new vision of my life to emerge that is for my highest good and the highest good for all."

Day 12–13 Be Intentional with Your Mouth and Thoughts

Choose freedom by speaking the Manna Mindset Manifesto (see "Days 1–2").

Meditate for 15 minutes.

Choose your words wisely and stay aware of your thoughts. Keep lifting them up to see your life and circumstance in the best positive light. Focus on the good. If you catch yourself saying or thinking something negative, stop and try to find a way to positively reframe the negative comment. If you just said. "I'm so stupid." Stop yourself and say, "I'm learning, and I respect myself for trying."

End your day by stating the affirmation for intentional speech and thought:

"I give thanks to the Universe for all the good in my life. I see everything working out for my highest good."

Day 14 Rest and Relax

Day 15–16 Elevate Your Mood/ Raise Your Frequency

Choose freedom by speaking the Manna Mindset Manifesto (see "Days 1–2").

Write down ten activities that typically uplift your mood, such as exercising, singing, dancing, walking, connecting with loved ones or nature, and watching or listening to something humorous or heart-warming.

Engage in these ten behaviors that lift up your mood throughout the day and create a sense of physical well-being.

End your day by stating the affirmation for raising your vibrational frequency and elevating your mood:

"I am available to more joy than I've ever felt. I accept the good and I am magnetic to love, prosperity, and good health!"

Day 17–18 Expect Miracles

Choose freedom by speaking the Manna Mindset Manifesto (see "Days 1–2").

Meditate for 15 minutes.

Create a sense of positive expectancy by training your thoughts to expect the best.

Do one thing on your list of ten activities that uplift your mood (see "Days 15–16").

End your day by stating the affirmation for miracles:

*"Things are always working out for me. I have
experienced miracles and I will again. I know the Universe
will find a way."*

Day 19–20 Act "As If"

Choose freedom by speaking the Manna Mindset
Manifesto (see "Days 1-2").

Meditate for 15 minutes every day.

Move forward in your life as if everything were
indeed unfolding for your highest and best good. Act
"as if" you are healthy, safe, loved, happy, and
prosperous. Claim that for yourself and create a sense
of certainty in your body. Then, take wise, not
reckless, action from that place today. Do what you
would do if that was your truth. See your life that way.
Feel it.

Do one thing on your list of ten activities that
uplift your mood (see Days 15–16").

End your day by stating the "act as if" affirmation:

*"I am [insert whatever you are claiming for
yourself here]."*

Day 21–22 Stay Present and Follow the Flow

Choose freedom by speaking the Manna Mindset
Manifesto (see "Days 1–2").

Check in with yourself every morning and throughout the day and ask: "*What do I feel called to do now? What is mine to do today?*" Let your action be authentic and guided by this moment rather than commitments, "shoulds," "ought-tos," and obligations.

Do one thing on your list of ten activities that uplift your mood (see Days 15–16").

End your day by stating the affirmation for staying present and in the flow:

"*I am present in this moment. I allow my energy and attention to flow to where it best serves me and others in this moment.*"

Day 23–24 Open Your Heart

Choose freedom by speaking the Manna Mindset Manifesto (see "Days 1–2").

Meditate for 15 minutes.

Identify activities that help you open your heart and keep it open. This might mean looking at kitty, puppy, or baby videos. Make a list of seven activities that you can do to open your heart and schedule that in your day. Do one activity a day that opens your heart every day for the next seven days.

Do one thing on your list of ten activities that uplifts your mood (see "Days 15–16"). *Hint:* If it opens your heart, it can be a two-for-one.

End your day by stating the affirmation for opening your heart:

"I open my heart to love. I feel deep love for myself, my life and my loved ones."

Day 25 Day of Rest

Day 26–27 Rest and Play

Choose freedom by speaking the Manna Mindset Manifesto (see "Days 1–2").

Meditate for 15 minutes.

Do one thing on your list of seven activities that open your heart (see "Days 23–24"). Schedule a 30-minute break to rest or do something fun and playful. You can use this time to express yourself creatively, as long as it you're not engaging in something structured that you're seeking approval for. Yes, it can also be something on your list of ten activities that uplifts your mood (for example: dancing, singing, listening to music).

End your day by stating the rest and play affirmation:

"I allow my mind and body to rest and rejuvenate. I allow myself to feel at peace. I exercise my right to simply be."

STEP 5: EMBODY MANNA CONSCIOUSNESS

You're in the home stretch now. You've almost completed the 30-Day Manna Challenge.

Day 28–29 Embody Manna Consciousness

Choose freedom by speaking the Manna Mindset Manifesto (see "Days 1–2").

Meditate for 15 minutes.

Do one thing on your list of ten activities that uplifts your mood (see "Days 15–16") and one on your list of seven activities that open your heart (see "Days 23–24").

End your day by stating all nine affirmations you used in Step 4 to create the manna mindset. (The complete list of Nine Fundamental Affirmations can be found on page 195.)

Day 30

Today, you will choose freedom again by speaking the Manna Mindset Manifesto.

"I choose freedom. I am a sovereign being, free from enslavement. I have a direct connection with the Source of all life. The Universe is my source and sufficiency in all things. All of my needs are met by the Universe in perfect timing. I receive manna from heaven daily and I am grateful."

Review the conditions or situations you felt challenged by that you wrote in your journal on days 1–2 and summarize your feelings and experience with these same conditions or situations now.

What was your experience with the 30-Day Manna Challenge? How has it impacted your experience with those situations? How are you different now? How is your thinking different? How has your experience changed? What experiences of manna did you have? How did manna show up in your life? Did you see how having gratitude and positive expectancy shifted your experiences? Did you identify your negative mental habits? Did you learn how to break your mental chains?

AFTERWORD

Thank you again for coming on this journey with me. Please take whatever works for you and remember that in every moment you can choose sovereignty. You can choose to align with manna consciousness and make the Manna Paradigm Shift.

In the Resources section you will find books and workshops to support you in your journey towards freedom and abundance. I wish you luck on your journey.

THE NINE FUNDAMENTAL AFFIRMATIONS

For Surrender:

"I am open to the Universe to bring forth my answers."

For a New Vision:

"I allow a new vision of my life to emerge for my highest good and the highest good for all."

For Intentional Speech and Thought:

"I give thanks to the Universe for all the good in my life. I see everything working out for my highest good."

For Raising Your Vibrational Frequency and Elevating Your Mood:

"I am available to more joy than I've ever felt. I accept the good and I am magnetic to love, prosperity, and good health!"

For Miracles:

"Things are always working out for me. I have experienced miracles and I will again. I know the Universe will find a way."

For Acting "As If":

"I am [insert whatever you are claiming for yourself here]."

For Staying Present and in Flow:

"I am present in this moment. I allow my energy and attention to flow to where it best serves me and others in this moment."

For Opening Your Heart:

"I open my heart to love. I feel deep love for myself, my life and my loved ones."

For Rest and Play:

"I allow my mind and body to rest and rejuvenate. I allow myself to feel at peace. I exercise my right to simply be."

ACKNOWLEDGMENTS

I wish to express my gratitude to the Great Spirit and to my spiritual teachers, some whom I shall name here: Myra Smith (Rest in Power), Estelle Frankel, Rev. Joan Steadman, and Rev. Michael Bernard Beckwith.

I want to thank my amor, Diana Martin Del Campo. Thank you, Love, for the numerous ways you support me and my endeavors. You've been a loving and generous cheerleader and your love has provided a steady foundation from which to give my gifts. Thank you for being my beautiful muse and personal gourmet chef.

Special thanks to my friend and colleague, Dr. Shefali Tsabary, who wrote the foreword to this book and who continues to inspire me with her spiritual depth and generosity since we first met in 1994. Thank you, beloved friend.

Big thanks to my writing colleagues who have read so many drafts of this book I'm sure they could recite pages by heart and who offered priceless suggestions and kept me moving forward: Adam Burch, Charmaine Colina, and Collin Watts, and my writing mentor, Philip Eisner who has kept me writing and believing in my writing for the last six years.

Gratitude to my spiritual community, especially Regina Gibson-Broome, Bianca Peters, Tunde Ilona,

Jennifer Amir, Gerald Wright, Jessica Colp, Lisa Chan, Stacy Harris, Laura Caputo, Jason Mitchell, Robyn Rice-Olmstead, and Gil Olmstead.

Special thanks to my support team: Margie Gordillo and Eileen Kenny and her healing staff.

Love and gratitude to friends: Tara May, Kristen Valus, Jilly Beccera, Karyna Garcia, Alice Lancefield, Gina Meyer, Gayla Turner, Karen Lambright, Audrey Borunda, Rachel McLaughlin, Martivon Galindo, Lynne Bartz, Mary Durst, Cory Nyamora, Mandy Benson, and Jenny Karns.

Many thanks to my publishing and promotion team: my editor and book packager, Stephanie Gunning, cover designer Gus Yoo, Kyle Pivarnik, Jane Brust, and Georgia Kolias at New Harbinger Publishing, who helped shape this material, and Caroline Pincus who supported this project.

Deep gratitude to my clients who have worked with me to *make the manna paradigm shift*.

Thank you to the following cafes where I spent hours writing pre-COVID: Basecamp and High Horse Dinette, Zweet and Lost Parrot.

And finally, deep gratitude to my parents, Janice Duchon and Rick and Louann Kotulski and my family: Barbara and Chuck Whitman, Abs and Amy Kotulski, Richard and Julia Baldwin, Ray Parker, Chloe, Dylan, Levi; Kathy, Scott, Cutter, and Davis Rudge, Luca and Dominic Leone; Vicki McKay; Alan, Jolly, Harvey, and Steve Kornicks; Shirley and Leslie Harrison, Marina,

Ryan, Ivan, and Kaleb Lenter, Juan Martin Del Campo and Christoph Korner, Elizabeth, Gene, Junior, Leah, and the Carranza Family.

NOTES

Introduction

1. Samuel P. Harrington. *Who Are We? The Challenges to America's National Identity* (New York: Simon & Schuster, 2004).

Chapter 1 A New Paradigm of Living

1. Marcus Garvey. "The Work That Has Been Done," a speech given on October 31, 1937, in Sydney, Nova Scotia.

Chapter 2 An Ancient Story of Liberation

1. This quote, said to Dr. Benjamin Rush on September 23, 1800, is printed on the dome of the Jefferson Memorial in Washington, D.C. From Thomas Jefferson. *The Papers of Thomas Jefferson, Volume 32.* J.P. Boyd, M. R. Bryan, L.H. Butterfield, and C.T. Cullen, editors. (Princeton, N.J.: Princeton University Press, 1950), p. 168. The sentiment has inspired generations of people; however, the tragic reality is that Jefferson was a slave owner. Although this was customary for

White men of his stature in that period of American history, the fact provides us little comfort today.

2. Jeff A. Benner. "Egypt," Ancient Hebrew Research Center (accessed October 19, 2020), https://ancient-hebrew.org/names/Egypt.htm.

3. Erwin Schrödinger. *What Is Life? And Mind and Matter* (New York: Cambridge University Press, 1967).

Chapter 4 Break Your Mental Chains

1. Roy F. Baumeister, Ellen Bratslavsky, Catrin Finkenauer, et al. "Bad Is Stronger Than Good," *Review of General Psychology*, vol. 5, no. 4 (December 2001), pp. 323–70, DOI: 10.1037//1089-2680.5.4.323. Also see: Amrisha Vaish, Tobias Grossman, and Amanda Woodward. "Not All Emotions Are Created Equal: The Negativity Bias in Social-Emotional Development," *Psychological Bulletin*, vol. 134, no. 3 (May 2008), pp. 383–403, https://www.ncbi.nlm.nih.gov/pubmed/18444702.

2. Ibid.

3. David Burns, *The Feeling Good Handbook*, (New York: Penguin Books, 1999).

Chapter 5 Connect with the Higher Mind

1. *King James Bible* (1611).
2. "Edgar Mitchell Quotations," QuoteTab (accessed November 9, 2020), https://www.quotetab.com/quotes/by-edgar-mitchell.
3. Ron Kaniel, Cade Masse, and David T. Robinson. The Importance of Being an Optimist: Evidence from Labor Markets," National Bureau of Economic Research, working paper 16328 (January 2010), http://www.nber.org/papers/w16328.
4. Andrew J. Oswald, Eugenio Proto, and Daniel Sgroi. (2015) "Happiness and Productivity," *Journal of Labor Economics,* vol. 33, no. 4 (October 2015), pp. 789–822.
5. Shawn Achor. *The Happiness Advantage: The Seven Principles of Positive Psychology That Fuel Success and Performance at Work* (New York: Currency, 2010).

Chapter 6 Surrender

1. Reinhold Niebuhr (1892-1971) wrote the Serenity Prayer in 1932 and it spread through churches and was embraced by Alcoholics Anonymous and other 12-step groups.

Chapter 7 Clear Your Mind

1. "Vipassana Meditation," Dhamma (accessed September 24, 2020), https://www.dhamma.org/en-US/about/vipassana.
2. Paul Grossman, Ludger Niemann, Stefan Schmidt, et al. "Mindfulness-based Stress Reduction and Health Benefits: A Meta-Analysis," *Journal of Psychosomatic Research*, vol. 57, no. 1 (July 2004): pp. 35–43, https://www.ncbi.nlm.nih.gov/pubmed/15256293.
3. Richard Chambers, et al. "The Impact of Intensive Mindfulness Training on Attentional Control, Cognitive Style, and Affect," *Cognitive Therapy and Research*, vol. 32, no. 3 (June 2008), pp. 303–22, https://link.springer.com/article/10.1007/s10608-007-9119-0.
4. Denise Mann. "Negative Ions Create Positive Vibes," WebMD (May 6, 2002), https://www.webmd.com/balance/features/negative-ions-create-positive-vibes#1.
5. Gaétan Chevalier, Stephen T. Sinatra, James L. Oschman, et al. (January 12, 2012). "Earthing: Health Implications of Reconnecting the Human Body to the Earth's Surface Electrons." Journal of Environmental and Public Health, volume 2012, article ID 291541 (accessed September 24, 2020), 8 pages, doi:10.1155/2012/291541.
6. Sunny Fitzgerald. "The Secret to Mindful Travel? A Walk in the Woods," National Geographic (accessed

September 24, 2020), https://www.national
geographic.com/travel/lists/forest-bathing-nature-
walk-health.

7. Kathleen Doheny. "Forest Bathing, Nature Time Are
Hot Health Advice," WebMD (June 11, 2019),
https://www.webmd.com/balance/news/20190611/fore
st-bathing-nature-time-hot-health-advice.

8. Shelley Snow, Nicolò Francesco Bernardi, Nilufar
Sabet-Kassouf, et al. "Exploring the Experience and
Effects of Vocal Toning," *Journal of Music Therapy*,
volume 55, no. 2 (summer 2018), pp. 221–250,
https://doi.org/10.1093/jmt/thy003.

9. Jonathan Goldman. "Sound and the Chakras,"
Jonathan Goldman's Healing Sounds (accessed
September 24, 2020), https://www.healingsounds.com/
sound-and-the-chakras.

Chapter 9 Elevate Your Mood and Raise Your Vibrational Frequency

1. Penney Pierce. *Frequency: The Power of Personal
Vibration* (New York: Atria Books/Beyond Words,
2011), p. xv.

2. As featured in the documentary *Heal*, written and
directed by Kelly Noonan Gores (2017).

3. "Exercise Is an All-natural Treatment to Fight
Depression," *Harvard Heath Letter* (July 2013, revised
March 25, 2019), https://www.health.harvard.edu/

mind-and-mood/exercise-is-an-all-natural-treatment-to-fight-depression.

Chapter 10 Expect Miracles

1 Jim Carrey. Commencement address, Maharishi University of Management (May 30, 2014).

Chapter 12 Stay Present and Follow the Flow

1. *Oxford English Dictionary.* Ed. J. A. Simpson and E. S. C. Weiner. 2nd ed. Oxford: Clarendon Press, 1989. OED Online Oxford 23, 2007.
2. Arnold van Gennep, *The Rites of Passage, second edition* (Chicago, IL.: University of Chicago Press, 2019), p. 21.
3. *King James Bible* (1611). Exodus 16: 2.
4. Ibid. Exodus 16: 3.
5. Ted Andrews. *Animal-Speak: The Spiritual and Magical Powers of Creatures Great and Small* (St. Paul, MN.: Llewellyn Publications, 2004), pp. 303–4.

Chapter 13 Open Your Heart

1. "The Math of HeartMath," HeartMath Institute (November 11, 2012), www.heartmath.org/articles-of-the-heart/the-math-of-heartmath/coherence.
2. Ibid.

3. Ibid.

4. Marcelo Campos. "Heart Rate Variability: A New Way to Track Well-being," *Harvard Health Blog* (November 22, 2017), www.health.harvard.edu/blog/heart-rate-variability-new-way-track-well-2017112212789.

5. "The Science of HeartMath," HeartMath (accessed October 23, 2020), https://www.heartmath.com/science.

6. Jessica Migala. "What Is Heart Rate Variability—and Do You Need to Know Yours?" *Health* (March 9, 2018), www.health.com/heart-disease/heart-rate-variability.

7. Ibid. Also see, HeartMath.

8. Campos.

9. Ibid.

10. "Chronic Stress Puts Your Heart at Risk" Mayo Clinic (March 19, 2019), https://www.mayoclinic.org/healthy-lifestyle/stress-management/in-depth/stress/art-20046037.

11. "Measuring and Practising Coherence—Heart Rate Variability," Tools Tips Techniques/HeartMath UK+IRL (accessed November 9, 2020), https://www.heartmath.co.uk/what-is-heartmath/#measure.

12. Rollin McCraty and Maria A. Zayas. "Cardiac Coherence, Self-regulation, Autonomic Stability, and Psychosocial Well-being," *Frontiers in Psychology,* vol. 5

(September 29, 2014), p. 1090, doi: 10.3389/fpsyg.2014.01090.

13. HeartMath.

14. Ibid.

15. Ibid.

16. Ibid.

17. Ibid.

18. HeartMath UK+IRL.

19. Liz Mineo "Good Genes Are Nice, but Joy Is Better," *Harvard Gazette* (April 11, 2017), https://news.harvard.edu/gazette/story/2017/04/over-nearly-80-years-harvard-study-has-been-showing-how-to-live-a-healthy-and-happy-life.

Chapter 14 Rest and Play

1. Lydia Saad. "The '40-Hour' Workweek Is Actually Longer—by Seven Hours," Gallup (August 29, 2014), https://news.gallup.com/poll/175286/hour-workweek-actually-longer-seven-hours.aspx.

2. J.G. Lu, M. Akinola, and M. Mason. "To Be More Creative, Schedule More Breaks," *Harvard Business Review* (May 10, 2017), https://hbr.org/2017/05/to-be-more-creative-schedule-your-breaks.

3. Jane Chertoff. "What You Need to Know About Active Recovery Exercise," *Healthline* (accessed October 23, 2020), https://www.healthline.com/health/active-recovery#benefits.

RESOURCES

You've made a great start at developing the manna mindset and embodying manna consciousness. For additional resources, please visit my website and take one of my workshops.

DavinaKotulski.com

Connect on the Social Networks

Facebook.com/drdavinakotulski
Instagram.com/drkotulski
Twitter.com/drkotulski
Linkedin.com/in/drdavinakotulski
YouTube.com/user/drkotulski

Book Recommendations

I'd like to gift you with a free download of an audio chapter from my earlier book, *It's Never Too Late to Be Your Self.* You can pick that up at https://www.davinakotulski.com/never-too-late-free-download.

If you wish to learn more about tangible political and social practices for sovereignty. I refer you to Sherry Mitchell's book *Sacred Instructions: Indigenous Wisdom for*

Living-Spirit Based Change (North Atlantic Books, 2018), where she discusses, among other the four foundations for self-determined society: food sovereignty. water sovereignty, energy sovereignty, and education sovereignty. These four foundations will assist you in remaining free from enslavement to outside sources.

Relaxation and Meditation Recommendations

For Jonathan Goldman's "7-Minute Chakra Tune-Up" audio download, visit his website: https://www.healing sounds.com.

I've found YouTube videos from Nature Healing Society and Spirit Tribe Awakening that share healing music with nature images in the background very helpful.

You can also check out the Mindful Moments Meditations on my YouTube channel.

ABOUT THE AUTHOR

DAVINA KOTULSKI, PH.D., is a licensed clinical psychologist, sought-after speaker, and award-winning author with a thriving therapy and international life coaching practice. She facilitates workshops and webinars on past-life regression, mysticism, meditation, spiritual growth, self-empowerment, and authentic living.

After receiving her doctorate in clinical psychology in 1996, Dr. Davina worked as a psychologist in a federal prison working to help inmates heal addictions and trauma and become productive members of society.

Dr. Davina received notable awards for her LGBTQ civil rights advocacy, including the Saints Alive Award from the Metropolitan Community Church, the Michael Switzer Leadership Award, and Grand Marshal, San Francisco LGBT Pride Parade. As a respected leader in the LGBT equality movement, Dr. Davina Kotulski has appeared in dozens of documentary films, been a guest on television (notably on CNN) and on National Public Radio and the talk shows of numerous other radio stations, and has been featured in print publications, like *Newsweek, USA Today, San Francisco Chronicle, L.A. Times, Oregonian,* to name a few.

Dr. Davina has been interviewed on Good Morning La La Land, Wake Up to the Sound of Transformation with Michael Bernard Beckwith, and numerous radio shows, podcasts, and online summits. She was a guest therapist on the show *Please Understand Me* produced by Sarah Silverman. In 2020, Dr. Davina's past life regression work was featured on the Sky Life Channel and the India-based web-show *OK-tested.*

Dr. Davina's previous books include *It's Never Too Late to Be Your Self, Why You Should Give a Damn about Gay Marriage, Love Warriors: The Rise of the Marriage Equality Movement and Why It Will Prevail,* and the novel *Behind Barbed Eyes. Behind Barbed Eyes* was a Nautilus Gold Award winner in 2016 and a 2019 Reader's Favorite Finalist in Fiction Audiobooks. *It's Never Too Late to Be Your Self* won the 2018 Nautilus Silver Award in the category of Inner Prosperity and Right Livelihood, was a 2019 International Book Awards Finalist in the category of self-help, and was a Finalist in the 2020 Next Generation Independent Book Awards in the Motivational Self-Help category. Her written work has been featured in periodicals, anthologies, online magazines, and blogs.

ABOUT RED INK PRESS

Founded in 2016, the mission of Red Ink Press is to uplift our readers with inspirational and entertaining fiction and nonfiction that empowers them to move beyond fear and perceived limitations to be their best and highest selves and create a world where love prevails. Our catalog includes books in the categories of personal growth, self-empowerment, spirituality, and psychology.

At Red Ink Press, we are committed to supporting authors who have a powerful message to share through their stories of transformation and redemption. Our aim is to feature characters and give voice to topics that are underrepresented in mainstream media.